'I can do many things in my life but if I do not fulfil the purpose for which I was sent it will be as if I have done nothing.'
– Bob Proctor

Copyright © MMH Press
First published in Australia in 2024
by MMH Press
Waikiki, WA 6169

All rights reserved. No part of this book may be used or reproduced by any means, graphic, electronic, or mechanical, including photocopying, recording, taping or by any information storage retrieval system without the written permission of the copyright owner except in the case of brief quotations embodied in critical articles and reviews.

Because of the dynamic nature of the Internet, any web addresses or links contained in this book may have changed since publication and may no longer be vaild. The views expressed in this work are solely those of the author and do not necessarily reflect the views of the publisher and the publisher hereby disclaims any responsibility for them.

A catalogue record for this work is available from the National Library of Australia

National Library of Australia Catalogue-in-Publication data:
Where Is My Mummy / Carole Goodman

ISBN: 9781763658295

Where is my MUMMY?

BEING THERE WHEN THEY NEED YOU MOST

CAROLE GOODMAN

I dedicate this to my children, Peter, Karyn and Michelle. And to my grandchildren, Sarah, Daniel, Lana, Mackenzie, Adam, Matthew and James. And I leave it as a legacy to all the mothers of the world and their precious babies. Present and future.

To my husband,
Barry James Goodman

Thank You.

You have been by my side for most of my life,
4th October 1969 and you are still here today.

Always walking beside me, not in front of me and not behind me but beside me.

I love you more today than yesterday and I will love you still more tomorrow.

I will always love you.

THANK YOU SO MUCH.
FOR BEING YOU.

'WHERE IS MY MUMMY?'

A long time ago, I don't remember when, but I remember these words – Where is my mummy? – being etched deep in my heart. I remember saying to my husband, 'The day will come when these words will come to fruition.' Yes, and I know *now* is the time.

I know the *time* is now, the *hour* is now to write this book and to write these words. It is said, *there is a book inside every person waiting to be given to the world*, and my time is *now*.

For today, in our world, there are two of the most vulnerable sections of our community: the youngest and the oldest – those just born into this world and those on their way out.

The youngest and the oldest. Both desperately in need of the greatest need of every human being – *to be understood* and *loved*.

The youngest has not discovered their *mind* and are so vulnerable as to what is planted in their subconscious by the environment in which they find themselves, and the oldest who are in the process of losing their minds, often feeling invisible and helpless, with nothing to contribute. They feel they are seen as a burden to society and are thus robbed of the last wonderful precious years of their life.

And now we can add a third, our beautiful precious teenagers who are struggling between the two, trying to discover *who they really are.*

It is our responsibility to give our little ones every possibility to become the very best version of themselves today, and to leave each one of them with a world that allows them every opportunity to become the very best they can be, to become **the leaders of tomorrow**.

This truly is our responsibility.

And in the words of Mahatma Gandi:

'The true measure of any society can be found in how it treats its most vulnerable members.'

A FORWARD
by Cassandra Willis

When my good friend and inspiring Mastermind partner, Carole Goodman, reached out to me to ask if I would be the first person to read her book and to help her with initial editing, I was beyond honoured.

Carole had been keeping our weekly group of thinkers updated each week throughout her writing journey, and I knew that this was not only going to be the most incredible legacy for her children, her grandchildren, her future descendants, but a blessing and a gift for parents all over the world.

As I read her story, I couldn't help but smile, as I read about this astounding woman, her life, her mission, her growth and her love for her family. I have known Carole for several years now, but when you read a person's story, the understanding that one has for that person, takes on a deeper and more awe-inspiring level.

I learned so much more about her and her passion for helping others, than ever before, and my heart glowed with love, admiration and pride for this beautiful lady, who has so selflessly laid herself bare through her writing.

This book is an inspirational journey of self-discovery, motherhood, awareness, and alignment, which showcases the increasingly deep understanding that Carole has about life, love and family. She provides the reader with thought provoking questions and advice, which I know will expand their awareness and ability to emulate and become the parent that they have always wanted to be for their children.

Mothers have such a unique purpose, and they must learn to navigate this without a guidebook. There are no rules, no short cuts and no get out of jail free cards. It's a game of the mind, however, they don't always know how to control their thoughts in the right and certain way, in a way that allows them to operate in harmony with the universe, or to love themselves first, so that they can love their children in the best way possible. What's unique about Carole is her incredible awareness of, and burning desire to share, the principles of success with other mothers, and to enhance their journey in a way that has never been delivered before. This book will be a gift for any mother, to enable them to think and act as the mother they want to and can be.

Truth be told, I'm not a parent. That wasn't my journey in this life. But I had a great one!

As I read Carole's words, I imagined how much my mum would have loved this book, and I realised how similar they were, in so many ways. My mum was a powerhouse of a woman, and Carole is a force to be reckoned with. My mum loved, laughed and lived for her family, and Carole has done the same.

My mum left her mark on this world, and Carole is making hers.

What I know about mothers such as these two impactful

women, is that they never stop loving and caring, they never stop teaching and learning, they never stop growing and serving others.

They are our greatest gift, our most treasured treasure, our best friend forever.

My mum is missed every day, and I am so grateful for her and the amazing mother she was.

I am also so grateful for a friend like Carole in my life now. I know that she wrote this book in spirit, and it has reminded me that I never need to ask the question "Where is my Mummy?"

She is always with me. All I need to do is think.

TABLE OF CONTENTS

Chapter 1: Congratulations, You Are a Mum 1
Chapter 2: Genetics 4
Chapter 3: Environment 11
Chapter 4: Progressive Growth – Forever Forward and Upwards ...16
Chapter 5: The Conscious and Subconscious Mind 21
Chapter 6: What Is Self-Image? 28
Chapter 7: My Story 30
Chapter 8: Success 33
Chapter 9: Our Five Senses 37
Chapter 10: Our Higher Faculties 41
Chapter 11: Teenagers: Their Own Self-Image 55
Chapter 12: The Burnt Chop Syndrome 64
Chapter 13: Attitude 70
Chapter 14: Time 76
Chapter 15: Sleep 79
Chapter 16: Gratitude 84

Chapter 17: Praise 87
Chapter 18: Non-Resistance 91
Chapter 19: Sacrifice 95
Chapter 20: Forgiveness 99
Chapter 21: Who Am I? *103*
Chapter 22: Legacy 105
References 110
Author's Note 112
Acknowledgements 115
Understanding 118

Chapter 1
CONGRATULATIONS, YOU ARE A MUM

What a bundle of joy *you* hold in your arms, and, *yes*, you are this little one's mum. Flesh from flesh and bone from bone, knitted together in *your* womb over these last nine months. *You* hold the life of this child in your hands. *You* are its world. *You* hold the most important position in the whole wide world. There is no more important job and nobody who can take your place. *You* are unique. There is no one like *you* in this little one's life. Congratulations. I am so very happy for *you* and *yes, you* are enough.

It is not so much the question, *Am I* worthy *enough to fulfil this purpose?* but rather, *Is this* **worthy of me?**

Yes, yes, yes, you are perfect. Knowing this is *why I so love being a mum.*

It is the most unique experience in all of creation. Nothing can equal it. Everything pales into insignificance compared to creating a new *human being*.

What a privilege we women have, to be co-creators – yes,

co-creators. What an amazing privilege.

Nothing can be compared to being a mum. To giving birth. It is the greatest accomplishment of any human being to give life to another human being.

There are many accomplishments we women may attain throughout our lives, many hats we can and will wear, but there is no greater position we can hold than that of being a *mum*. It stands out as the greatest accomplishment of any human being. You do not need to be anything or anybody more than you need to understand *who you are* and know *you are enough*. Everything is inside you. No abundance of possessions, titles, money or anything in this whole world could ever replace or compete with *who you are right now*.

The most important and satisfying hat you will ever wear is the hat you wear as a mum. You are everything and have everything you need within you, right now. You have all the wisdom, understanding, counsel, fortitude, knowledge and love *within you*, and *you* are now the educator of this brand-new tiny human being.

You have the responsibility, or should I say the privilege, of *drawing out* of your child who and what they will become. The true definition of an educator comes from the Latin root 'educo'. Educate means to 'lead out or bring forth'.

It is already within your child, it does not need to be received from the *outside;* it already lies *within* your precious child, and you are their first and most important educator.

Your baby is unique, not all the tricks in the trade or artificial intelligence can create a human being. Nothing and nobody can duplicate your child. It's just not possible, because it is a unique spirit.

WHERE IS MY MUMMY?

The love you have for your child will guide you. Believe in yourself and trust your instincts and you can't go wrong.

When those beautiful baby eyes look at you with all the unconditional trust and belief in *you*, fill them with all the love, happiness, joy and belief you have in them and in who they are and what they are capable of.

You are their world, the only world they know and it is you who will guide them until the age of reason, when what you have fed them during these first few precious years will shape how they reason, with the information thrown at them from left, right and centre in the years to come, from the media, newspapers, television, books, teachers, friends, religious teachers and more. So, *yes* feed them all the *good stuff* so they are well-equipped with a healthy self-image and so much self-love, enough to be able to make the good decisions they will need to make, necessary for a strong healthy life, and can avoid being tossed around by their outside world.

You are their teacher of *today*, so they may be the *leaders* of their world *tomorrow*.

Then tomorrow we will have leaders who inspire their world. Leaders who know their self-worth and have self-love, comfortable with their own self-image. Equipped to lead their people, treating all people as they would have people treat them. Yes, leading with love and understanding.

Now let us look at this little one and understand how it came to be here in the first place and how their own individual genetics and their environment have impacted their little life right from the beginning.

Chapter 2
GENETICS

Biologically, we are a *masterpiece. We have been incredibly formed and gifted with the unique ability to co-create a new life.* We are just amazing and we, ourselves, have been created to fulfil what is the most *purpose-filled achievement in the whole world.* Truly there is nothing of more importance that has or can ever be created which can compare to this achievement, uniquely designed for *us* women.

Our genetic conditioning goes back for generations, and for our little one, the most recent being, when a little particle of energy from Mum and a little particle of energy from Dad came together and, woo-hoo, became our precious child. Before that it was our mum and dad and before that our grandmother and grandfather and so on and so on. Yes, our child is the product of all the generations before them.

Did you know our ovaries were developed in our mother's womb, which housed all the eggs we will ever have? Then, when our mother was in our grandmother's womb, she too carried all the eggs she would ever have. The egg of *who* we are was planted in the womb of our mummy when she was born and before that our grandmother and generations before that. We are born with all the eggs we will ever have to bring forth life from within us.

And just to further reinforce how unique we women really are, did you know we females only release *one* tiny egg each month? Whereas the sperm from the male has millions of seeds, the successful seed fighting its way through to unite with this one tiny egg. How amazing and precious is that. I find it beautiful that sperm makes such an effort to be the *one* to reach this tiny egg. It must fight hard to be the victor, whereas we only release one precious egg each month.

This one biological masterpiece is enough for all women to realise how amazing they really are.

It took me a moment to truly understand this amazing journey of the sperm from the first meeting of this determined energetic single-minded sperm with this one tiny chosen egg whose joint destiny was to become a human being. When I finally understood this process, it left me speechless, for it truly is a miracle, starting way before conception.

Did you know that behind the scenes in the dark recesses of our amazing world of genetics, much preparation is at work? For we women, it began when we started to menstruate around twelve years of age, or even younger. A little later, our hormones came into play and we became physically attracted to someone who could potentially become a possible biological partner in this exciting journey of procreation. When the time was ready, everything started to happen. In the other field at play, there was a fierce competition going on. It was *the race of the potential sperm*. The most rewarding race with the most valuable prize to be won.

It comprised of the fittest strongest most determined little sperm survivor of his field and his aim was to be the winner of the race. This sperm had to be the best in his field because he had to withstand the efforts of all the other sperm challenging him for this most worthy prize.

Mind you, some of the other sperm lost the race and were not worthy competitors because they just lost their way, went the wrong way and others just gave up because it was too much effort. This is understandable because it is a very difficult and arduous process for sperm. This little survivor should be celebrated because he *never gave up*. He was the one who went on to co-create with the egg and ultimately produce another perfect human being.

This one biological masterpiece is enough for all we women to realise how amazingly unique special and worthy we really are, for this is the end of the physical work for the partner whilst the ongoing miracle for we women continues for roughly another forty weeks, or 280 days, at which time we have the almighty privilege of giving birth to another unique human being who has been entrusted into our care.

We often observe this in the world of nature and are astounded at the extreme efforts some species go to, to win over the affection of their mate but rarely, if ever, do we stand back and see ourselves in this role.

In our modern world, when we hear the word *genetics,* we tend to think of our own personal DNA; this marvellous tool of discovery which has revolutionised our understanding of our family history, where we have come from and the inherited blood that travels throughout our body. Knowing our biological history is so very important when we consider our health and what may have been passed down through our family history and that of our partner, parents, grandparents, great-grandparents etc. All of which may impact our health and that of our little ones.

However, it is my intention here to look at **who we are** in the context of *why* we do as we do and *why* we do not do as we want to do.

And therefore, the area of genetics I refer to here are the paradigms or characteristics which have the capacity to follow us through our lives and impact us from one generation to another.

One may hear it said, *You look like your mother, grandmother, aunty, etc.* You have the same colour hair the same eyes and, like it or not, your looks are often handed down from one generation to another.

However, what is even more important are the way genetics are passed down to us in a method often called *traits or paradigms.* In writing this book, I choose to call these paradigms, which when accepted can control our lives for the positive or negative. Paradigms are simply a collection of habits or thoughts, and can be seen in our creative faculties, sporting prowess, musical talents and in all areas of our lives. They can be seen as positive and negative. They are a very important controller in our lives, often creating our reality, and most of the time we are completely unaware of them.

I say these can be positive and negative, and these paradigms can be very insidious as they can control the way we live our lives, be it one of happiness and success or unhappiness and failure. These paradigms, if not understood, can follow us and control us until we reach our grave. Bob Proctor in his lectures on *The Success Puzzle* would suggest that:

'Your paradigms control your reality'

One such paradigm operated in my life until very recently and has had a vast impact on me. It's a shame when I am now seventy-four years old, and I only discovered it whilst studying my family history.

I had recognised from a young age that I had a 'chip on my shoulder', especially when I was being criticised, reprimanded, or given advice. I always felt slighted, and my 'back would go up', as they say.

I recognised my own mother also had this paradigm, and then discovered when looking through the family history, evidence of this same paradigm controlling the life of my maternal grandmother. I was shocked but at the same time grateful, for now I knew by recognising and addressing this area of my life, not only could I release myself and live a healthier and happier life, but I could also nip it in the bud for future generations of my family.

This awareness is nothing to be ashamed of; it is one of our most treasured gifts, and if we are open to becoming happier, more peaceful and self-loving human beings, we will rejoice and be grateful when we recognise these genetic unhealthy paradigms, setting ourselves free. It really is an exhilarating and beautiful process. Much healthier than ducking for cover and being imprisoned in our little world, living a life of denial for the rest of our days and, worse still, allowing it to be passed onto our next precious generation and beyond.

These paradigms can affect every and any area of our lives – be they in the area of, but not limited, to relationships, finance, health, success, education or perceptions – yes any and every area of our lives.

Genetics are also very important as they have a big impact on our health, and therefore on the health of our little one. Health, whether good or not so good, is often an inherited state of our biological parentage, passed down from one generation to another. In my family, my dad had an unhealthy heart and died when he was sixty years old. This heart condition was passed onto me, however with better awareness and understanding, coupled with modern day progressive advancement in medical science, my generation is now in excellent health.

Hence, we can see how our genetic history does have a great impact in our lives and those of our child and therefore plays a major part in our lives.

This leads me to another significant mover and shaker in our lives, and therefore the lives of our little one today. It lies in the *environment* into which we and our little ones are born.

I never thought much about environment until recently. I do remember discussions around nature verses nurture in my distant past, but honestly, it did not mean much to me until I came across the amazing Bob Proctor, who spoke and taught about this in such a simple and understandable way, that even children can understand it.

I became quite upset and even angry when I listened to his explanation of the understanding of our environment into which we were born and then raised, especially in our formative years, and how this environment has the potential to have a greater influence than genetics in our lives, and therefore in the lives of our little ones.

Extraordinary, you may say, and this is also how I felt. My first reaction was, *Why wasn't I told about this earlier in my life?* A bit rough to finally get an appreciation of its importance when most of my life is over. However, I am ever so happy and grateful now that I know.

So how about we take a look at what we understand to be our environment from K Meninger in the book *You Were Born Rich*, page ten, (1997) by Bob Proctor:

'*Environment is more important than heredity.*'

Chapter 3
ENVIRONMENT

James Allen, in his book, *As a Man Thinketh & Other Timeless Works,* page 185 (1903) wrote:

'Man is mind and, evermore he takes the tool of thought, and, shaping what he wills, brings forth a thousand joys, a thousand ills; he thinks in secret, and it comes to pass: Environment is but his looking-glass.'

So here as we examine the importance of *environment* in the development of the early minds of our little ones, I truly believe that.

The environment is but their looking glass.

Yes, truly, our environment, which is made up of our parents, grandparents, teachers, community, friends, religious teachers and anyone who has had access to our formative years – yes, anyone or anything that has had access to our most powerful mind – has really been the one in charge, and this is called our environment.

In today's world, none has become more influential in the formation of our minds and our thinking and those of our children and sadly our present-day teenagers than the media. As wonderful as technology is in our world today, and I truly believe it is, it also has the capacity to take control of our minds.

It is by us taking back the control of our minds, through *awareness and understanding* that we as mums come in.

First, let me explain. I am not talking about the environment as thought of through the lens of climate change or nature. Whilst these areas of discussion have their importance, I believe what we are talking about here goes beyond anything that is on the table of world importance *now*. The environment we live in has direct control over how we think, what we think and, ultimately, the results we have in our lives. This is important to grasp, as the whole world, the world we all occupy, is controlled by our thinking, and now as we come to understand it, it is not always our thinking that is controlling us, but the outside world that is feeding our minds. Indeed, it can be said, we are like robots being controlled by the outside world.

Those who come to understand this and use it will control their own environment and have the capacity ultimately to control the lives of people all over the world.

Much has been understood about the importance of and influence of the environment in which we have been brought up, and the area of psychology covers this most effectively; however, there is one very particular area which properly understood, could, I believe, be the most important and effective address to the social behaviour of our young people today, and it lies within the hands of we *mums*. It lies with our awareness and understanding.

The environment in which we have been brought up in, and that of our children, is so very important. I don't believe we really understand the impact our environment has had in the past, but once understood, many things fall into place.

The little minds of our children are open to anything and everything you and their environment put into it. You can tell them a lie or a truth, you can tell them anything you wish, and they will believe you, absolutely. And you may say, *Who cares? Children don't know the difference* – but this is where the damage comes in. You may think they will not know the difference now, but it all goes into the treasury of their mind and is taken as gospel for the rest of their lives. People often ask, *What is wrong with teenagers these days?* Or, *Why did they do that – they should know better?*

Yes, it is the environment we are born into, the environment in which we were raised. Our parents, extended family, society, schooling, friends and our culture. All of these are our environment, and they have been instrumental in shaping and moulding us. We are now allowing the environment surrounding our little ones to control them as well. It is influencing the minds of our little ones, and it is these thoughts flowing into their little minds that form their thinking. The *most influential* impact on who they become happens from conception until the tender age of reason.

YES, we are programming our child's mind, every moment of every day and whatever is going on around them and coming in through their five senses, what they see, hear, taste, touch and smell, is imprinted on their conscious mind which then flows into their subconscious mind and becomes *truth* to them.

This information will be the *thinking* they live with when they grow up. No wonder so many of our young people have such a difficult start to their lives, with some of the most abusive behaviour given, knowingly and unknowingly, to them during these formative years of their life. We are their examples, and they believe everything we say and do.

Talk to your child as a *thinking human being*. Always let them know their opinions matter. Never allow other people to make them feel *invisible*.

Parents of today need *courage*. Courage to stand alone when they need to go against popular trends of *thinking*. Remember, the environment is the looking glass from which our child views its world. What they see you do and how you think and act, is how your child will see and interpret things. This is so very important to understand.

Not everyone will agree with you and pat you on the back. Your family, friends and society in general may think you are giving your child too much attention, and say you are spoiling your children. They may even say, *What does it matter, they will turn out the way they will anyway?*

They are not being unkind, they are just being ignorant and unaware of how important the impact we make in the lives of our little ones, that will have a dire impact on their future as teenagers. It is too late when we turn around in ten years' time and ask, *What is happening to my child? Why does my child think and act this way?*

With growth comes discomfort. You need to be willing to outgrow your peers, your friends and even your family if you are going to live a fulfilled and happy life, living on your terms, breaking old cycles of *thinking* and choosing a new path. Hopefully they will grow with you and support you through your journey, but worrying about what others think about us during this growth is not our priority or problem. Indeed, what others think about us is really none of our business and if we allow it to worry us, then that is our choice. Our attention should be fully focused on what and how we think ourselves, and subsequently how our thinking affects our child.

Yes, time passes quickly, and we only have our children for such a short time, so the impact we have in forming their little minds, their **self-image**, the lens through which they view their world and the world which they will gradually find themselves in, is so very important.

Most mums, whilst in the middle of raising a demanding little one, will think at times, *When will they ever grow up?* I remember this so well with my own children. I remember a time when my children were young, and I was in my local shopping centre, observing to myself, *Most of these people must have had young children at some time and they managed to live through it. How did they survive?* This thinking seems so dramatic now, but it was ever so real back then. And I did survive, and I did have great kids, but the challenges were real. I only wish I knew then what I now know. But no-one can ever get back time. When it's gone, it's **gone**.

Chapter 4
PROGRESSIVE GROWTH – FOREVER FORWARD AND UPWARDS

Human beings from the moment of conception are always in an upward progression.

Think about it. From the very first moment the seed and sperm connect, they begin to multiply over and over again, without us even knowing it. This tiny being is alive within us. It continues to grow and expand every second of every day, until the day it is born. Then it keeps on expanding and growing in fuller expression in mind, body and spirit, day after day after day until their last breath is taken.

We witness this in the womb and rejoice, becoming absorbed with this progression of our baby's physical growth. We often fail to see this operating as a natural progression in their mind and spirit as well. Many people tiptoe through life hoping to arrive safely at their grave, not really understanding that living the fullness of life which is continual *'expansion and greater expression'*, is meant to continue for the rest of their lives. The enormous milestones achieved by our babies both within the womb and then in the first few years of their life are meant to continue for the rest of their lives in mind, body and spirit.

Isn't it interesting how we glorify our achievers? Yes, we sit in cauldrons and cheer our heroes on, and this is evident in our world of sport today. We are so emotionally involved with the success of our sports people. The whole nation, if not the world, idolises our sporting heroes. We cheer on those who want to run faster, jump higher, swim faster and play harder. Achievement is what it's all about.

And yet, if we stopped for a moment and processed what our little ones achieve in their first few years of their life, we would be astounded, but we take it for granted because it is seen to be the *norm*.

Yes, our little ones achieve all their milestones, and we continually tick off these accomplishments one by one as they happen, for most of us, not realising that these accomplishments underpin them for the rest of their lives. We sit back, and for the most part, *we take it all for granted.*

The first five years of a baby's life are considered to be their most informative years, and when we look at the advances they make during this time, it stands to reason why we think this to be so.

From the moment they are born, a baby is always learning, little by little and continually discovering their world. From the moment they leave the protective warm cave of their mother's womb, where every need was met, and are then plunged into the unknown where they have to trust their needs will be met, dependent on another human being who is *you*, they start discovering their universe. Their bodies automatically breathe, sleep, process foods, eliminate waste and grow automatically. They cry when they have a need, be it hunger warmth or security, and when their basic needs are met, they then begin to focus on the world around them.

- They discover they have little hands and feet, sometimes by biting their toes, and in doing so, realise they are attached to them.
- They start to discover their little world and the people around them, Mummy, Daddy, etc.
- They have an urge to move. They take their first chances in life irrespective of the consequences, first by crawling, then by standing and swaying on their feet and eventually, after many failed attempts, by trial and error and persistence, they learn to use those little legs they have, and they take off and walk.
- They learn to eat from a spoon and eventually with a knife and fork. They learn to sip from a cup and eventually drink a whole glass without spilling it. In doing so, they have to discover first where their mouth is, what fun and games they have, and once having accomplished this, it will be a joy for them for the rest of their life.
- They hear and then learn to speak, and we are their teachers.

And on and on it goes, discovering and learning forever,

expanding and more fully expressing themselves. Yes, it is the beginning of a lifelong journey.

However, often, we die long before our physical body dies because we have given up seeing the joy of life. Our lives are meant to be forever *expanding and progressing,* however, because many of us think we know all there is to know, and live just to *get by,* we end up dying long before we physically die. How sad when we were born to grow, grow and grow forever, expanding and fully expressing our gifts and talents, adding value to others in our marvellous world.

I have heard it said that a minister at a funeral once shared that the saddest part for him when officiating at a funeral, was not the passing of the person who had died, but the death of all the unfulfilled dreams locked up inside of that person, who often has *'never really lived'*.

Nature is one of our beautiful teachers, even weeds will grow through cement to find sunlight. This thirst for expansion is a continual progress in nature and is built into us as well. I will often talk to a plant which is struggling to survive, and it is wonderful to witness how the garden then grows. Oh, yes, it is so beautiful. If nature can do it, so can we.

The reason we consider these first five years to be the most informative is because our children are absorbing all they are exposed to, there is no *reasoning* happening in their little world. The age of reasoning was once thought to be around seven years old, however it may be much sooner than this. It is during this window from birth to five or seven years that anything that is fed into our child's mind is accepted with no resistance. This is why it is important to be aware of what we allow our child's mind to be exposed to.

Often, this material will stay in our child's mind for the rest of their life, and they will continue to operate from the beliefs they have accepted from the teachers around them, be they negative or positive, because until the age of reason, they accept whatever they are exposed to and have no ability to reject it.

To have a better understanding of this, let's take a look at our beautiful mind and how our thinking actually runs our lives, and will run the lives of our little one forever.

Rather than go through life mechanically we need to understand how important our thinking is in our life, probably more important than anything we will do in our life. And *DO* is the operative word, as *thinking is an action*. It is like the navigational system in our car, our 'Sat Nav', it gives *direction* to our lives.

Earl Nightingale, in his book *Lead the Field*, would suggest, 'We become what we think about all day long.'

Chapter 5
THE CONSCIOUS AND SUBCONSCIOUS MIND

Now the question you may be asking could be, *Where is our mind?*

When I say the *mind*, what do we immediately think of – most people would point to the brain. However, the mind is not the brain. The brain is an electrical system, the greatest ever created or ever will be created, but it is not the mind. *The brain is the mind's instrument.*

The reason most people believe the mind resides in the brain is perfectly logical, as man has never seen the mind. That is because it is not an organ, it is *energy*, and it flows throughout our whole body even to our fingertips. Nobody has ever been able to see it, however, it really is the most visible part of a human being, as it can be seen in every thought, every action, every response and every result in every person's life. Yes, every single person.

As previously explained, nobody has ever seen the mind. If I asked you what colour your car is, you would immediately see a picture of your car come up in your mind and you would see the colour of it. This same question could be asked about your front door, your kitchen or your favourite dress. However, if I asked you what your mind looked like you couldn't tell me. This is very important because, as I stated before, it is our *mind* that controls everything we think, say and do. Ultimately, it is the actions we then take which bring about the results we get in our lives.

Pretty awesome and somewhat scary at the same time. All thoughts enter into our conscious mind which is our thinking mind and then these thoughts, if unchecked, automatically flow into our subconscious mind, which, believe it or not, has no ability to accept or reject; it is completely deductive. It will believe everything we tell it. It has no ability to differentiate between a lie or a truth.

In this beautiful amazing incredible world in which we now live, the age of what was once unimaginable has become the norm. We have sent men to the moon and brought them safely home, discovered quantum physics and made discoveries in medical science that would make your hair curl, yet what stands before us today, and every day for every one of us, is our incredible mind, which most of us just stand by and let any thought flow into it, with little understanding of how it works.

The mind is the pure magic of which the story of *Aladdin and His Magic Lamp* adhered to and what Napoleon Hill spoke about in his incredible book, *Think and Grow Rich*.

'*What your mind can conceive and believe it can receive.*'

It's why some people appear to have it all. For some, everything turns to gold, whilst others are always struggling.

WHERE IS MY MUMMY?

It seems like magic for those who do not understand how the mind works and how amazing it is, but it is not magic at all, for magic is only magic until we understand something.

So let us have a look at this mind; both how the conscious and subconscious mind work.

We are born with a *subconscious mind*, often referred to as our *emotional mind* and this is where our feelings reside. All the information from our little one's outside world is fed into the subconscious mind, whether that information is good, bad or indifferent.

Our conscious mind, often referred to as the *thinking mind*, develops when we are about five years of age, and this is considered to be our *age of reason*.

This conscious mind has the ability to accept or reject the information fed into it; it is said to be inductive. This is important to know because it is where every thought and idea we have flows into. If not checked, it then flows into our subconscious mind which is totally deductive and has no ability to reject. It accepts good and bad, healthy and unhealthy, a lie or the truth, as the conscious inductive mind has allowed the thought to flow through into it.

We must understand that when raising our little ones, the conscious thinking inductive mind has not yet been formed. To reiterate this once more, this does not happen until around the age of five to seven and is known as the *age of reasoning*. This is why it is of absolute importance that we only feed good healthy positive thoughts into our little one's subconscious mind. We have the responsibility to raise our child and there is nothing of more importance than to fill this little one's mind with positive, loving, encouraging, healthy happy thoughts of themselves and their potential as this will form their *self-belief and their self-love which will then form into self-image.* Later, when the conscious mind develops, it will reason out what it can pass onto the sub-conscious mind.

The conscious mind stands as a guard and as we *think* it sifts through what we believe and what we do not believe. If the sub-conscious mind has been fed with limiting and negative thoughts up to this point, the conscious mind will accept those kinds of thoughts as acceptable. Interestingly, we usually continue through life *not thinking*. As adults, we *think* we are aware of our thoughts, but in actual fact, most of the time our thoughts are not vetted and slip through, whether they are good, bad or indifferent. Therefore, we allow anything to flow into our conscious mind and then all this information from our conscious flows into our subconscious mind, and since the subconscious mind has no way of rejecting what is fed into it, it does not know the difference in what we see as real or unreal, we lay ourselves open to continually feeding our precious subconscious mind with all harmful information that causes worry, fear, stress, unhappiness and even sickness. These negative thoughts dominate our thinking and this has the potential to make our lives very different to what we would love them to be: calm peaceful happy healthful and, literally, living in abundance, as life was always meant to be.

Unfortunately, we have never been taught this, so now, we as mothers of the next generation are also ignorant and totally unaware of what we pass on from one generation to the next.

Our parents and grandparents are not to be blamed, as they did the very best with the knowledge they had, but now we have a better understanding of how the mind works, we can use this knowledge to create a better world for ourselves and the next generation.

We now know that what we teach our little ones will forever have an enormous impact on their lives.

We can teach them how to guard their thoughts so they can be the master of their lives, and to understand that what they feed into their precious minds does actually control their lives.

If we do not come to grips with this understanding now with our own children, we will follow in the same footsteps as our parents and those before them. This is one of the most important things we must come to understand, because this is where most of our beliefs are born. They are planted in our subconscious minds when we are little ones, and they become our *truth*, be it a good belief or a negative belief.

Our children as babies, our little ones, taking everything we do and say as gospel, directly into their subconscious mind, without having the ability to vet this material, it then impacts their thinking and belief, often for the rest of their lives.

Remember, there are:

Little Eyes Upon You - Author Unknown

There are little eyes upon you,
and they are watching you night and day,
their little ears that quickly take
in every word you say.
There are little hands all eager

to do anything you do,
and a little person who's dreaming of the day
they'll be just like you.

You're that little person's idol,
you're the wisest of the wise,
in their little mind about you
no suspicions ever rise.
They believe in you devoutly,
and hold all that you say and do,
they will say and do it your way,
when they grow up just like you.

There's a wide-eyed little person,
who believes you're always right,
and their eyes are always opened,
and they're watching you day and night.
You are setting the example,
every day in what you do,
for the little person who is waiting
to grow up to be like you.

Believe it or not: *you* hold your child's future in your hands.
You shape their future.
Now we can see how important environment is, as it impacts our conscious and subconscious mind, therefore it is imperative to understand this when raising another human being. Along with their physical advancements, it is equally important what is fed into their beautiful minds. Always open, always watching,

soaking up what they see and hear around them, through their five senses, being whatever they see, hear, feel, taste and touch, are forever scanning their environment and accepting whatever is fed into their subconscious mind to be *true*. This will forever impact their life and be in control of their future. It is how they view their world for, their environment, is their looking glass.

CHAPTER 6
WHAT IS SELF-IMAGE?

We have already discovered that our babies are the product of someone else's thinking until they reach the age of *reasoning*. They depend on us, their mums, for the first early years of their life and we are their guard, the keeper of their little mind. Everything they see, hear, smell, taste and touch is going into their little mind, through their five senses, whether it's good, bad or indifferent. It is our responsibility as their mums to be the guard at the door of their mind.

And yes, I can hear you screaming, *But how can I do this?* Well, the good news is, it really is not hard, no not hard at all, really quite simple. It all comes with understanding, then using your awareness and love.

Understanding *what*?

Our own self-image. This is formed on our inside, and as we have now seen, it is initially formed by our genetics and then the environment in which we live.

WHERE IS MY MUMMY?

Self-image is 'how we see ourselves'. However, this is often muddied by the misconceptions that are operating in our lives. It is interesting to discover that most of our thinking is from the outside in rather than the inside out. Do you realise that most of us operate from a concept we are not even aware of? When I heard this, I was shocked. The concept of who I am comes not from *who I think I am* or *who you think I am* **but** *who I think you think I am*. This is what controls so much of our thinking, and unless we recognise this concept operating in our lives, this will be the perimeter we will always operate from. It is impossible to have a healthy self-image with this belief running the show in the background.

Understanding this allows us to become clear and ask: *Who is really telling me who I am and therefore running the show of my life? Is it the 'environment' I grew up in and surrounds me now, or is it ME? Do I really own my self-image or is my self-image based on who I think you think I am, as well as what I've been told I am by those who loved me the most? Is it the outside world telling me who I am?*

The secret of all successful people lies in a healthy self-image. It is formed in the people who go far in life. The 'overcomers', who face the challenges and obstacles that come up along their journey, but never quit or give up. People who do not blame their circumstances for the things that happen to them; they get up and make their own circumstances. People will call them lucky and make excuses for their own unsuccessful lives, but success lives within each one of us, and we only need to recognise it and say *yes*. I believe the saying, ***I can*** opens more doors and is more important than IQ.

CHAPTER 7
MY STORY

It is 23 July 1970 and I have just become a mum. The most exhilarating, emotional, happy day of my life. I have given birth to a beautiful healthy 8lb 4oz baby boy, but I had no idea, that I had no idea, of the gift I had been given. It would take me fifty-two years before I began to truly understand.

I was on cloud nine that day, and I remember being transferred to the recovery room in the maternity ward of our local hospital and sharing the experience with another lady who had also become a mum. The nurse came in and told us to be quiet as there were other people in labour nextdoor. I couldn't help sharing that I was in 'seventh heaven' and what a wonderful place to be; what a beautiful experience to be a mum, there is nothing like it in the whole world.

I remember thinking my baby was the most perfect human being ever born, and how right I was. My baby was unique and once again *I was right*. I thought I would be the perfect mum – **wrong**.

I am a mum and have no earthly idea what I'm doing.

I had no real understanding of *who* lay before me; the most amazing incredible intelligent perfect human being. Of course, every human being is born perfect with the potential to be, do and have everything they were created to be, do and have. Each one of our babies are placed within our hands to bring out this potential but so few of us know this or how to do it.

My children could not have been more loved. They were great kids, and today, the one common thread running through each one of them, is, that their hearts are always open to add value to the lives of other people in their world. They are all community-minded, each in their own professions, and I am happy and grateful for them.

Still though, I wish I had known then what I know now. If only I had understood who I was holding in my arms, extraordinary human beings with the most amazing incredible mind, body and spirit, and I was the mummy of these children.

Yes, I did all the *'physical'* things expected of me. I went through the ritual of feeding them the right foods, got them into a good sleeping pattern, bathed them and even made toilet training in record time. In many ways I could have ticked all the boxes to be 'Mother of the Year' but I wish I had truly understood and had an awareness of the amazing 'gifts' I had been given.

I would have spent the time to *just be with them*. Yes, I was 'present' physically and, to some extent, emotionally, however I had no understanding of the potential they had and how I was responsible for bringing this to the fore. Pouring the understanding into them and telling them just how perfect and precious they were, feeding them the understanding of the potential within them and filling them with all the good stuff.

There are the practical things to do which are important, but we need to understand and become aware of exactly what we are doing and how to fill them from the start with a healthy self-image. Yes it starts at the beginning. There is time enough for everything else. Take the *time,* this precious *time,* to fill up their tank with this understanding *now*.

We get one run at this. This is not a *practice run*. We do not get a *second chance*. Today is today and then it's gone.

I am still grateful I brought my first baby home to where I lived with my mother-in-law. She steered me through the first nine months of my baby's life until my little family moved into our bright shiny new home, some distance away in Camden, NSW. There, I was all alone and had to rely on my basic understanding to bring up my child. Ironically, our second child, a beautiful daughter, was born some two years two months and ten days after our son. I say this as ironic because two years two months and ten days later we became parents once again to our third beautiful child, another daughter, born in Brisbane.

I was twenty years old when I gave birth to my first baby, and in those days, it was a normal age to be married and have children; that was life back then. I thought I knew everything I needed to know to raise my incredible little child, however I never gave it a thought that it was my *responsibility* to raise this child. I alone am *responsible,* it really is up to me to bring up this child; a child that will, hopefully, grow up with a healthy self-image, equipping them to be in charge of themselves and make the right choices for themselves in the years ahead.

CHAPTER 8
SUCCESS

When we hear the word *success*, we immediately associate it with something we are familiar with. This can be in the sporting arena, where many of our heroes are found. Or in the world of academia, where often, the more you can remember is acknowledged. Or perhaps the world of science, for which we are forever grateful for because of the wonderful advancements and discoveries we are the beneficiaries of in our world today. Or the amazing world of the arts or politics. However, very few acknowledgements are made to the most important job in the world, and that is raising a new human being.

Earl Nightingale in his insightful book, *Lead the Field,* describes success as: 'The progressive realisation of a worthy ideal.'

The understanding of this wording can be misleading, as it is not asking you if *you* are *worthy* of this *ideal,* but rather, is this *ideal worthy of you.*

It is of critical importance we understand this, as we are trading our life for this ideal. That is what being a mother is all about. I believe once we understand this, we are on the road to *success.* Earl

Nightingale continues to use this principle in regard to receiving *compensation* for something one has done. He goes on to suggest the three requirements necessary to receive compensation for what you do, and when studying these requirements, I couldn't help but wonder if these very same principles are required within us mums, in order to make us a successful mother?

These three requirements are:

- The need for what you do.
- Your ability to do it.
- The difficulty in replacing you.

So, let's think about this for a moment, as I believe everyone looks to be *successful* in life and there could be no more important perspective for a mother, to be able to look back and say, ***I am a success,*** *I have brought up another human being who has a wonderful strong healthy caring mindset, contributes to their community and is always progressing in all the areas of their life.* To me, that is *success*.

I cannot think of any other more valuable advancement in our glorious world than the importance of bringing up human beings who really understand *who they are* and work with this amazing thing we call our ***mind***. There could be no more worthy ideal than to bring up another healthy happy human being who adds value and happiness to this beautiful world.

Now let me explain how these three principles for *success* apply to you as a mother.

- **The need for what *you* do:** Giving birth and bringing up a human being is the most important **need** of all time. The world is nothing without human beings. Without human beings this world would just be a stage set for a movie with no actors in it. This is the first reason I decided to write this book, so that you may realise how important you really are.

- ***Your ability to do it:*** This is the crux and the second reason *why* this book has been written. We must be equipped with every available tool to guide us as in how we can understand and have the awareness of how to be the educator of our precious new human being, and that they may grow into their fullest potential. And *yes* we need to know and *believe* we can do it.
- ***The difficulty in replacing you:*** Reason three was because I wanted *you* to know there is *nobody* who can replace *you*. And to reinforce to you – *you are enough*.

You are not duplicatable. There is nobody like *you*. And there never will be. *You* are the only mum who can meet your child's needs.

I can say now, *I did fit this bill.* I couldn't see it then, but looking back now, I realise I just didn't know it. And you know what? *you*, yes you, are the one who can also say yes. You *do* fit this bill because you tick all the boxes of being a mum to your child. There is no-one in the whole wide world who could fill this need in your child's life. There is no-one else who could have more ability than you, because you alone are this child's mum. *And* there is no person on this planet who can take *your* place.

There is a need *now* for what you are doing. A desperate *need*.

We are looking at a generation where many of our teenagers

are lost and lonely, searching for *who they really are*. Trying this, trying that, listening to those who do not have the answers. It is sad to see precious teenagers in our society, *lost, lonely and crying out for help,* not understanding who they are and the incredible potential within them.

You have all the *ability* required when they are in their formative years. *You* are their mum and the only limits in our life are those we impose upon ourselves.

No-one can replace *you*. And as we are beginning to understand this, we all have the ability we need to apply it in the lives of our future generation.

When the going gets tough – and it will – remember nothing worthwhile is ever accomplished without some effort.

But is it worth it? *Oh yes*. You see, you can never go back and repeat this precious time that is *now*. For now is the time you have and now is when the sowing is done, for tomorrow is the reaping time, but without the right seeds being planted, the successful reaping will not happen. Hence today is important. It is all happening *now*. So, it is *now*, today, that we choose to give to our child the very best start to their marvellous life. The foundation starts *now*. Tomorrow may be too late.

We have been asleep, and we must wake up and see the power we have within us, taking responsibility for ourselves and that of our child, the human being we have chosen to bring into this world.

Again, I can hear you screaming out, *But how do I do this?* My answer is through awareness and understanding. So, take a little journey with me as I explain the things I did not know. Remembering to be gentle with yourself as you go along, as this is a journey.

CHAPTER 9
OUR FIVE SENSES

Most of us understand we have been born with our five senses. These generally can be observed in how we live our lives and the manifestations we bring about through our health, happiness and prosperity.

They are essential to our wellbeing – good and bad – and once again we have the choice to use them however we wish.

They are:
- Sight.
- Hearing.
- Taste.
- Touch.
- Smell.

To *taste* fine food, to *feel* a beautiful hug, *smell* the perfume of a rose and to *hear* music of our favourite band or the sounds of our favourite orchestra. Or gaze on the most beautiful *sights* this amazing world has to offer. Yes, we are born with our five senses, and life is beautiful. As we watch our child awakening to these senses, we treasure each moment and marvel at our child's development.

The first time our child opens their eyes, we believe they know us, the first time they smile we know it is the sweetest smile we have ever seen (even though people try and convince us it's only wind). The moment they utter their first word – be it 'mumma' or 'dadda' we claim it as a recognition of us. Every step they take, crawling, standing up and walking, all the developmental stages of their little lives, we are overjoyed by these 'normal and natural' progresses in their life and can't wait to show our family and friends the next important step our child has mastered.

It is our five senses, though, which really do control our lives. Often, we are not aware of it. As we saw before in understanding our mind, our five senses draw everything into to us from the outside, everything that is going on around us. Our senses pick up everything, without us vetting much of it at all. The music we hear, the media we watch, be it the television or the newspaper we read. In today's fast-moving world, we spend little or no time *thinking*, let alone *choosing*, what we allow to be fed into our precious minds. And don't forget, what we feed into our *minds* is who we become. What an extraordinary thought – **we are what we think about** – therefore we should be doubly careful what we allow to flow into our minds, and especially what we allow to flow into the precious minds of our little ones.

Everything we hear and see is very important. We just do not see it until the fruits of these senses are manifested, and we can now see the examples of this in the lives of our teenagers today.

One only has to look at the ads on the TV from the fast food outlets, and we almost salivate when they are placed before our eyes. They make it so easy for us with 'home deliveries', to make our lives even easier, so we don't even have to leave our living rooms. How easy is that?

The *smell* of KFC is just so delicious, I can hardly resist it, and they tell me how good it is for me. So here I am, using my senses of taste, smell, hearing, seeing, and yes, even touch because I get to hold it in my hands and feel the joy of anticipation. How do I stand a chance?

I love home deliveries, in the sense that I don't have to go to the supermarket where I am tempted to overspend on all the foods that weren't on my list but somehow ended up in my bags when I arrive home. However, we must learn to choose when, where and what is working in our lives and what is working against us.

Touch is one of the most important senses for our wellbeing. Most of us don't realise how important this sense is to our growth. Indeed, children can suffer from a lack of touch, referred to as *infant neglect,* it is caused by deprivation of touch. It can, in extreme cases, prevent a baby from developing a healthy stress response and even stunt growth. We teach our children from an early age to be good little go-getters, but rarely do we encourage them to be good little go-givers. Teach them to give hugs and spread love and happiness, and it will come back to them.

Take a moment, go outside and find a beautiful flower. Bend down and smell the unique perfume that has been given just to them, through nature. Smell their perfume through your marvellous sense of smell. Not out of a bottle made in a factory with someone's brand name on it, but the free original smell gifted to you by nature. Nature is such an extraordinary factory, the likes of which can never be duplicated.

We could not survive without our five senses, gifted to us when we were born. We need to be grateful for them, and begin to use them as an ally, not as an enemy. Presently, the evidence we see in obesity, teenagers running amok and people living in destitute situations are evidence of these beautiful gifts being used against us.

We often sit ourselves down in front of the television, sometimes for hours on end and allow the media to run our subconscious. We rarely vet what we are watching. Be observant of all the negativity you are allowing to literally pour into our conscious mind. People will say, *I need to know what is going on in the world,* and this is true, however, be aware of how you respond to this news. Does it leave you in a happier, calm, loving place or are you stressed, anxious, fearful and worried? An example of this is when the financial reviews come on the screen of our television, and it is predicted that we are going into a slump, or maybe they are expecting a recession to hit us soon. How do you feel? Be guided by your ***feelings*** as they are a sure way of knowing what you have allowed to control your *thinking*.

As James Allen said in his book, *As a Man Thinketh*, 'Man is mind and evermore he takes the tool of thought and plants it where he wills. Brings forth a thousand joys, a thousand ills; he thinks in secret and it comes to pass. Environment is but his looking glass.'

To come to an understanding that we have allowed our five senses to control our lives, is important for our health and well-being, and it will flow onto our children, yes, the next generation.

However, do you know your child has also been gifted with six other incredible gifts which we call their **_higher faculties._** We, the parents, probably have absolutely no inkling of them. Most of us do not even know we have been born with them, so how could we understand our children have them? However, it is our responsibility to develop them from within.

CHAPTER 10
OUR HIGHER FACULTIES

Today, a beautiful package has arrived at your front door. It's the prettiest package you have ever seen. All wrapped up in gorgeous paper and tied with a big bow and it is addressed to you.

Your heart is singing with joy as you carry this pretty parcel into your living room, and as you sit down and pull the ribbon, your excitement, anticipation and expectation is hard to contain. You open the box and, inside, six little boxes sit there all each individually wrapped just for you.

These six gifts are for you, and they are the most precious gifts you will ever receive. However, they are, a belated birthday present; belated simply because you received them on the day you were born but maybe you have never opened them until NOW. This is because you need to unwrap them and use them. They are your *higher faculties*.

These *higher faculties* contain the greatest power in the whole world, and they lie within us, though very few of us have ever heard of them, let alone *used* them. It is almost frightening to know the power we have within us. Do you know the gifts you have within – the gifts you were *born* with?

I did not either, and when I started 'unwrapping' them, I was both astounded and angry. Why wasn't I told of these before? So, let us now unwrap these beautiful gifts we were given on the day we were born.

OUR HIGHER FACULTIES

We operate from our five senses but hardly know anything of our higher faculties. Our five senses really do have control over our lives.

We have been taught through ignorance to build ourselves from the outside in, through our five senses rather than the inside out, through our higher faculties. Crazy, isn't it? However, if we come to understand our higher faculties and how to use them, we really will become the master of our lives, the captain of our souls. Yes, *we* will be in control.

THEY CONSIST OF OUR:

- Imagination.
- Will.
- Reason.
- Memory.
- Intuition.
- Perception.

IMAGINATION

We build through our imagination and, then, through repetition we make it happen.

This higher faculty literally gives me 'goosebumps'. It is always seen by the little ones but rarely is it understood by the *grown-ups*. Yes, we parents think we know it all and the **imagination** is something we 'grow out of' as we mature. How misunderstood this concept of imagination is. We truly have been robbed.

Napoleon Hill, in his wonderful book *Think and Grow Rich*, recognised that: *'Imagination has been said to be the most marvellous, miraculous, inconceivable, powerful force the world has ever known.'*

And truly this is so. Imagination is the starting point of all inventions. It starts as an idea in the mind. It might start with the pots and pans in the kitchen cupboard, but if it is not nurtured – or worse still, if it is *stopped* through ignorance – it may forever be killed off.

Do you ever dream? Do you ever take yourself away and dream about what *you* want? What you *really* want? Do you build castles in the air as you did as a child?

Do you? Generally, most of us have never done this in our adult lives. Most probably, we've never even thought about doing it. Certainly, it was not encouraged in us, and it's fairly safe to say, we have never been shown how to use this amazing gift. You can decide to start to dream … now.

Many of us can probably say, *Hey, I remember when I used to play imaginary games as a kid, but I soon grew out of them.* We played cowboys and Indians, doctors and nurses or my favourite teacher and the students. Oh yes it was so much fun. And were we not transported off to some *imaginary* place, until we were snapped back to reality and told to, *Stop daydreaming and pay attention.* And the dream was gone. After many, many times of having our imagination 'disciplined', we soon started to let it go, and one day it was gone, and we were told daydreaming is for children. That is when I supposedly 'grew up'.

No … that is when the dreams I had died.

Never dampen – or worse still, *kill off* – the dreams of your child. You kill off their dreams by saying things like, *Who do you think you are? You could never do that. Where do you think the money is going to come from? Money doesn't grow on trees you know. Be realistic, you could never do that. Don't build yourself up for disappointment.* And, *Only really smart people could ever do that. Just be satisfied to get a regular job, one that will bring in a pay cheque each week.* And if by chance we did have a dream and voiced it, we were often told, *You're getting too big for your boots. Now you are building castles in the air.* The extraordinary thing is that much money, time and thought was spent buying the very things that those who loved us the most set about eventually to destroy.

We were bought all that was needed so we could fly in our imagination to the moon; the fairytale books, the fire truck, the doctor's kit. All this transported us off to our beautiful imaginary world. We do the same thing with our own children. We take them to Disneyland, which encourages them to use their imagination. We take them to see all the beautiful Disney movies. Yes, and then we kill off all the dreams they've been creating with our own limiting negative thoughts, beliefs and actions, until dreaming, using their own wonderful imagination, slowly disappears. Yes, we build them up just to let them down. However, know we really can't kill off these 'higher faculties', for they can never die, but they can be stopped and remain dormant for the rest of their lives.

There have always been those who were the 'dreamers'. The exceptional few who never stopped daydreaming. And for these we owe our deepest gratitude. Yes, many of our marvellous inventors, those who would not let go of their dreams, who persisted no matter what, even though they were often misunderstood.

Thomas Edison, who dreamt of harnessing the energy of the universe and after ten thousand attempts discovered the 'incandescent light bulb' that now lights up cities all over the world and brings the light into our homes.

Guglielmo Marconi, the Italian inventor who dreamed of a system for harnessing the intangible forces of the ether. He is instrumental in bringing information into the very households of our community today through wireless radio, which was to pave the way for television, computers, hand-held phones and the internet.

The Wright Brothers believed they could build a machine that would fly through the air. They believed they could sustain an aircraft in the air, and they did. Now we fly all over the world in their wonderful machines.

Rae Kroc, after delivering an unusual supply of milkshake makers to a small business in California, run by the McDonald brothers, caught a vision of duplicating these stores all over America. *yes*, that grew into what we know as McDonald's today.

The great Walter Disney who fed our imaginations and invited us to dream. Thank you Thank you so very much. We truly can dream and let our imagination fly.

None of these inventions, which today we consider *normal* in our modern world today, came about without vision, daydreaming, persistence, discipline and courage over many years, whilst often being, misunderstood, ridiculed and ostracised.

One could go on and on, but these inventors used their magnificent imagination to bring these ideas into the lives of all of us today.

We need to read to our little ones the stories of the *dreamers* who encourage them to *dream*. Listen to their dreams, their imagination at work. Always make the time to listen to their imagination. As you tuck them into bed tell them stories, yes make them up, about themselves and how strong, courageous, talented and smart they are. Always make them the hero, never the extra in their story. This will grow a belief in them and over time it will form the most valuable and essential beliefs about themselves. Their very own magical amazing incredible **self-belief**.

WILL

The *will* is our ability to *focus*.

'I see only the objective, the obstacles must give way'

This was a quote by Napoleon Bonaparte, the French Military Commander and political leader during the French revolution. Marshalling the power and bringing it to the *will*, is the secret of all successful people. Concentrate on one thing at a time, to the exclusion of everything else. Oh, my goodness. isn't this so evident in the lives of our little ones when we watch them at play. The utter concentration to the exclusion of everything else is amazing and yet so often, we try to interrupt this amazing concentration with the view that they are being disobedient and choosing to ignore us.

This focus will, in time, become the basis of having the ability to make a *decision* quickly, and stick to it, which is said to be the platform of every successful person. Very often *the will* is thought to be something one has to 'crush', especially in a child, as we consider them being disobedient when, in fact, it is something we need to encourage, so they are not will-o'-the-wisps or procrastinators. Their ability to make a decision and stick to it grows as they are encouraged to complete a little aspiration which will in time grow within them, an ability to follow through to the end in whatever dream or project they invest themselves in. The pride and self-belief this grows within our children is the beginning of courage, which is necessary for when they need to listen and believe in themselves, when some future decision-making in their lives becomes hard.

The *will* is what has always carried successful people throughout the ages.

In June 1962, when John F Kennedy, the then President of the United States, asked the renowned scientist, Wernher von Braun, what it would take for him to fly men to the moon and bring them safely back to Earth, he was given a very simple answer: *'The will to do it.'* It is the will, the passion, the desire to do something that carries that something to completion.

Think of Henry Ford who dreamt of an eight-cylinder engine and set his workman the task of creating it. They kept coming back and saying, 'It's impossible,' and he kept sending them back to the workshop and telling them not to come back until they found it. Finally in 1932, they broke through and brought this invention to the world. It revolutionised the automobile market and made it available to everyday men and women, then and today.

We would not have the technology we have today without the sheer will and persistance of amazing people.

Look at sport, and see the likes of Roger Bannister, the first to run the *'four-minute mile in under four minutes'*. This had been previously considered impossible, as it was believed the human body was incapable of running so fast.

It was with his sheer will and persistance that he first broke the record on 6 May 1954, in Oxfordshire. Yes, it is the *will* that makes these, and all other progresses, happen in our world.

Used constructively, it truly is one of the greatest faculties we have and so often we destroy it in our children because we strip them of *their will* in our attempt to discipline and control them.

INITUITION

Intuition is one of the most interesting and least understood of our higher faculties, simply because it is illusive. It is not tangible, we can't see it, as it is often invisible as to be ignored, or if we do see it, we are told, *That is stupid and why would you think that?* Or worse *feel* that? Well, I will tell you why – it's because we as adults have not had this faculty fostered from within us. Instead of understanding this as 'in-tuition' – exactly *tuition* from *within* – it has been brainwashed out of us. Mainly only animals and children still use this faculty.

Why is it that an animal, any animal, can use their *intuition* to decide whether a person is to be trusted? A dog, for instance, will attack a person who is afraid of them, quicker than a person who lives in harmony with them.

Yes, this higher faculty is one of the most beautiful gifts one could cultivate in our children, one which will guide them throughout their lives. Be wise and listen with your heart to their, and your, instincts.

Many believe prayer is us talking to God and *intuition* is God talking to us.

Many of us may think we have lost this gift, but it is never *lost* as our higher faculties are part of who we are, and we just need to understand them and *use* them. It may take practice. However, they are there, and they are to be used.

PERCEPTION

Perception is another one of my favourites for it is how we view the world. It navigates us on our journey through life, and the best thing of all, is that we have the ability to choose to change our *perception* if it is not serving us. How incredible is that? *Perception* is simply our point of view. It just *is*.

The use of this one higher faculty has the potential to bring peace to our beautiful world. Understanding and respecting the *perception* of other world leaders, respecting where they are coming from and truly listening to their hearts has the potential to break down the barriers that divide us and bring us into a place of true peace and harmony.

We see it in our own families, siblings growing up in the same environment, but both having a different perception of the same situation. Not necessarily right or wrong, just different, because everything just **is**.

One can be in the company of family, friends or fellow workers, sitting around chatting, one conversation is centred on the joys of the world and all the beauty they see in their environment, while others will only share of the ills they see in the world; conflict, lack, disappointments, hardship. You will know by the way you *feel* which one is edifying and which one leaves you with a feeling of lack of energy.

Ask yourself, *Are you uplifted by the conversation or are you left with anxiety, worry, fear and negativity?* Yes, you will know by the way you feel.

Choose your environment wisely and gauge it by the way you feel. Remembering all the time that everyone has the right to their own opinion and each opinion just *is*.

When you open this gift, you open up a whole new world. This is going to be *your world* and it really is up to you, now, how you wish to *view your world*. Remember, each person is entitled to their own *perception* of things, nothing is right or wrong, and we must allow people to have their own perception. Let people be free to live their lives the way they want, just don't allow others to steal your energy.

Some people will walk through life with 'rose-coloured glasses' and only see the beauty in everything and everyone. Others will always find something wrong. Both coming from their own perception. Same situation, different lenses.

Most of us can go through life digesting the opinions of other people and making them our own. Hence, it is so very important that we 'have a good and sound conviction of why you do as you do and how you think as you think'. ~ Earl Nightingale.

I will always remember my granddaughter when we went into the city for a day out with the family. We had travelled by train, and after a lovely day, we were making our way to the train station when it began to rain.

We adults responded with the normal dismay and annoyance at getting wet, and then my granddaughter, who was four at the time, came out with, 'Oh how beautiful the rain is, it will now water Grandmum's garden.' Having just spent time in the garden the day before replanting some garden beds, she could only see 'good' in the rain.

If we could take a lesson from children and look through their eyes and just enjoy life, how much simpler it would be.

My own children continue to teach me this lesson as I sit and listen now to their *perception* of things that happened in their childhood. Each will see things differently and neither is right or wrong – just different. So interesting.

Ralph Waldo Trine in *In Tune with the Infinite* would support this – in his words: 'For nothing is good or bad, our thinking makes it so.'

MEMORY

Everybody has a perfect *memory*, and we normally use it through ridiculous association. When I say we all have a perfect *memory*, think of it like a muscle in our body, and if we don't use it then we generally will lose it. If we break our arm and it remains in a sling for a while, it will need exercise to bring back the strength of the muscle. Our *memory* is just like that; we need to *use* it. As good as our technology is, it is also taking over our ability to work things out for ourselves in our memory bank. I will generally reach for my phone for an answer to a mathematical equation, where once upon a time I would have it worked out in my mind as quick as a flash. It really comes down to *using* our memory.

There are many ways in which we use our *memory*. First being the memories themselves. Those memories of yesteryear that so captured our imagination, were stored in the 'memory box' of our mind. Too precious to throw away and forget.

We store them in our *memory* and visit them often and particularly more so as we age. It is such a delicious activity to remember the precious times and activities of our journeying through life. It is when we start to forget, as we age, that it becomes apparent we are losing our memory faculty. The happiness, the joy, the sweetness of our good memories of past days gone by.

Another use of *memory* is as a tool. Through this we remember what we learnt. That which we added to our memory from studying, be it through ongoing education or skills we develop throughout our life, tools for us to make a living. This *memory faculty* allowed us to expand ourselves and continue to more fully express ourselves, and it has accompanied us on our journey through life. Often, this avenue of *memory* is facilitated through the use of repetition.

This is so applicable to our system of learning in school. I was brought up the 'parrot' fashion way; it was called the 'rote' method of learning. Each morning, we were taught the 'times tables', and consequently we got a wrap on the knuckles when we got it wrong.

Yes, we learnt quickly and now, at my ripe old age, I can tell you the answer of any multiplication from 1x1 to 12x12. Yes, that is one way of teaching,

Now, I resonate more from this way of thinking which was given to me by Bob Proctor: *'When one learns by remembering they will most often forget. But when one learns through understanding. They will never forget.'*

When I see my grandchildren cramming for an exam, I encourage them to *understand* what they are trying to learn, and when they grasp it, they will never forget.

Often, our children will be given a certain piece of material to learn and then they are judged on the ability to remember this for a particular subject, at a particular time, on a particular day, and if they are having an *'off day'*, they are marked a *'failure'* with a big red X. This really is not a true indication of their ability, it is only testing their retention capability at that particular time on that particular day. What they really need is to remember through understanding and application, and in this way they will truly be building the muscle of the *memory faculty*.

REASON

Reasoning gives me the ability to think. Not to necessarily take things that people say and run with it. But to think it through and, as it suggests, *reason* things out for myself.

It is the ability to accept or reject what one understands to be truth to themselves, having good and sound reason for what they believe to be true. Our little ones use their reasoning factor when they ask, **why?** That word sets up such an emotion of frustration in us and sends us crazy at times. Don't fob them off with 'just because' as an answer. Explain why. Little ones are a mass of intelligence, they only lack experience and vocabulary.

Nothing can make me think what I don't believe to be true. *Reasoning* gives me the ability to accept or reject things for myself.

However, another way of reasoning is what I describe as 'the way of the heart'. This is often seen as illogical especially when the weight of information gathered, goes against the grain as one would be heard to say. Children are no different; they can actually 'feel' when you are fobbing them off with a lie.

Reason is not always based on conclusions made with logic. It is about *choosing* what we want to accept and that which we want to reject. Originating new and exciting ideas. We are talking about the *'faculty of reason'* as the ability to *think,* really *think,* and be forever open to changing those ideas which don't sit right with us anymore. It is so important to be prepared after 'thinking', to throw away 'old thinking' that does not sit right with us anymore and is not serving us or is unhelpful to our growth.

This works just the same in corporations as well as in the playground at kindergarten, or amongst siblings at home.

I love this thinking of Ralph Waldo Trine (1897) *In Tune with the Infinite*

BEAUTY IS WITHIN

Loving friends! Be wise and dry
Straightway every weeping eye;
What you left upon the bier
Is not worth a single tear
Tis a simple sea-shell, one
Out of which the pearl is gone.
The shell was nothing, leave it there.
The pearl – the soul – was all, is HERE.

At first, I was a little taken aback with this *thinking and reasoning*, however, upon reading this, over and over again, I saw the beauty in it. We live in a physical body which is awesome, but we also have an inner self which I call *spirit,* and it is this that I see as the *pearl*. The physical body being the outer shell.

When we die, our physical body will disintegrate, but our *soul* our inner self remains. Whatever happens to our soul is open to one's own beliefs. I believe the spirit never dies and this is comforting as our loved ones continue on in some form or another. The body will die and disintegrate but the spirit lives on.

We are made up of our body, mind and spirit. That which is our physical body may be gone but we are spiritual beings, and we only reside in this physical body. It is the heart, the spirit and the mind, within each one of us that makes us who we really are.

That what is seen as our physical bodies is only the house that contains our spiritual beings.

The true beauty comes from within; it shines from within. The true beauty comes from the heart and mind.

CHAPTER 11
TEENAGERS: THEIR OWN SELF-IMAGE

Much talk is being made of, *What has happened to our teenagers of today?* We are in the early 2020s and our politicians, teachers, parents, law enforcers and now even the victims of crime are all asking *how we can address this reckless behaviour* that is not only destroying the fabric of our society as we have known it in the past, but more importantly, destroying our teenagers of today, who are our leaders of the future.

Many years ago, when I heard this catch cry which struck at the core of my being *Where is my Mummy?* it was predicting the time would come when our future teenagers would rebel and would have no idea *why* they were rebelling … and that day has come. I do believe many of our wayward teenagers of today are crying from the heart, **where is my mummy?**

Our teenagers of today are the product of many changing experiences we have lived through over the passing decades, and like any generation, these experiences have left their mark.

The years of WWI and WWII left their mark on the teenagers of that time, many being robbed of the presence of their fathers mentally, physically and emotionally, and lived with a continual fear playing out in their lives through the uncertainty in their world at the time.

Many of our teenagers today have a different ache in their lives; it is called *lack of a healthy self-image*. They have been brought up with what has been known as the 'technological age', where for many of them, the media has brought up our babies.

Why is it so much of a surprise that our teenagers are running amok, when for most of their formative years we have *unknowingly and without blame* (as we cannot know what we have not been taught ourselves), allowed our little ones to be formed by the outside world and outside influences? The television was their babysitter and now the media is their – and our – influencer. My heart breaks for our beautiful teenagers who have not had the opportunity to discover who they really are.

Yes, we have this amazing wonderful life-changing tool in our lives and we are blessed and grateful to the pioneers of this industry for gifting us with this life-changing tool but that is exactly what it is – *a life-changing tool* – and if we do not choose to be the master of it today in our lives, and the lives of our little ones who will become the teenagers of tomorrow, then it will be the master and controller of both our lives and that of our future teenagers forever, just as it is in the lives of so many of our teenagers today.

I am so very happy and grateful for technology and how it has enriched my life. I have the awesome opportunity daily to keep in contact with my children and seven grandchildren, something parents of previous generations did not have access to, however, where technology was once a *servant* in our lives, it has now become the *master*.

Our teenagers of today are now at the mercy of it, and if we do not choose to do something now, it will continue to be the master of their lives forever. Now is the only time we have. The lives of our teenagers lay in our hands **today**. *Wake up and reclaim their lives, the lives of our present-day teenagers and that of our future generation of teenagers.*

Where is My Mummy? is being written from a burden I have carried for a long time, and it cannot stay unwritten any longer.

We ask, *What can we do with our teenagers of today?* I would suggest we teach them an understanding of how their mind really works and then build within them a beautiful self-image by giving them inner eyes to see *who they really are* and the incredible potential and power within them. Yes, change the present self-image they have of themselves and teach them of self-love and self-care. Only in this way can we have any hope of saving many of our teenagers of today.

We do this by working with the conscious and subconscious mind which melts and moulds a new and beautiful *self-love, self-worth and ultimately a new self-image* within our beautiful teenagers.

It is also of the greatest importance, that we take care of the mind of our babies of today, so they become the healthy, happy, loving, caring teenagers of tomorrow. This is **why** this book has been written. Really love and saturate them with a great self-image from day one – or better still, before they are born, when they are in the womb, for they really can hear us. Build wonderful self-love and self-image in them, a beautiful belief of *who they* *really are*. Speak to them now of how you see them as a teenager of tomorrow. For they really are our future leaders.

Help them build a beautiful positive self-image that is kind, seeing only the good in others. Happy, generous, forgiving, supportive and compassionate, because they have been blessed with an environment of people who hold these ideals for themselves and have passed them onto their children, and therefore onto a generation who understand they have a mind and, most importantly, know how to use it to create the world of their dreams.

Always remember each our teenagers of today is a **person**; a product of the environment in which they are raised. They don't just 'pop out' at fourteen, twelve or even as young as ten years of age and become a teenager. They have been groomed since before they were born, the environment they choose to associate with now, and almost all of who they believe themselves to be now is tied up within what these past environments had them believe themselves to be.

Have they been brought up in an environment where they were told, *You are beautiful, smart, amazing, honest, capable of doing anything you set your mind to, the world is your oyster, you are kind generous and loving*? Or have they been brought up with these words ringing in their ears and mind and ultimately their heart, *You are lazy, good for nothing, you will never amount to anything. You are always in trouble and can't be relied upon for anything, I wish I never had you. Get out I never want to see you again*?

I remember years ago a family, who went to school with my children, was attending a function I was involved in, and I was conversing with the mother of the three-year-old little girl. During our conversation the mother interrupted me and said,

WHERE IS MY MUMMY?

'Excuse me, Carole, Rebecca wishes to tell me something.' I remember well the thoughts and feelings that went through me. I remember looking down and seeing this child and thinking, *You are a child*, almost as if she was invisible, and then thinking, *How could you have anything of importance to say*? I was dumbfounded and astonished how this could happen. Now I understand why she and her siblings became the captains and top students in the school, achieving great success in their lives. The confidence, high self-esteem, great attitude and kindness these children displayed in their teenage years was due to the self-image instilled in them in their formative years – yes, the environment they grew up in.

If a healthy self-esteem, self-love and self-image has not been formed before they reach their age of reasoning, and then nurtured through to their pre-teens, they may well be influenced by the environment they choose to associate with. Their environment is not only those they associate with at school and their leisure hours physically, but in today's world, just as importantly through the media, Twitter (X), social media etc.

This becomes their world, be it positive or negative. If our teenagers have a positive self-image they have a good chance of choosing their way of life. Others who have not had this advantage may well become sheep, following others around them. 'Following the follower'. They are conforming to one another and that is the problem. They are going nowhere. Lost and searching for answers that are just not there. How tragic.

The subconscious mind is always ensuring that what it 'believes' is 'true'. Hence, what it has been told, is what it manifests. By its very nature, it must believe what it believes to be true. Irrespective of whether it is actually truth or not. Hence, our teenagers become what their subconscious mind tells them who they are, and this is what their environment – yes, the environment they were brought up in – told them about themselves, who they were and what they were capable of doing and becoming. This is not to say our environment was necessarily bad, but many of we parents have been taught to raise our children in much the same way as our parents and others who impacted our subconscious. Not that they did not love us or did their very best, however they were only doing what they themselves were taught to do and so on and on it goes.

Remembering how the mind works, how our conscious and subconscious minds work, now we know how necessary it is to have a new awareness and understanding of how our teenagers have been programmed.

One of the most important ways teenagers have been programmed started in their childhood. It was when we didn't allow them to *'make a decision'* for themselves. We rarely asked them what they thought. It is such an important stage of their growth to make their own decisions. Maybe, a better response could be, *What do you think?* This allows them a degree of independence and will give them confidence to make more positive decisions for themselves in the future.

Many of our teenagers are desperately searching for this understanding in their lives today, and we, as the educators of the next generation, have the responsibility of programming this into the minds of our teenagers of tomorrow. I pray and trust this understanding and awareness will also flow into the systems that surround our teenagers today.

The American moral and social philosopher Eric Hoffer (1902-

1983) once observed: *'In times of change learners inherit the earth; while the learned find themselves beautifully equipped to deal with a world that no longer exists.'*

We are now, and have been for the past two generations, in a *period of change* where the learned ways of responding to non-acceptable behaviour are just not working, they are obsolete. It is the learners in our society, those who understand and have an awareness of what is happening within our teenagers, who will make the necessary healthy changes so peace and harmony is restored through a greater self-image and self-love and self-respect our teenagers can take their rightful place as the future valuable leaders of our world tomorrow.

The education system, the judicial system, the leaders of our churches, the media, which is one of our most influential teachers of our teenagers today – Twitter (X), Facebook, Instagram – all those powerful systems that already have control of our teenager's minds and hearts today, need to take stock of what is happening and take responsibility for the impact they are having on our teenagers, for the future belongs to them.

I can hear the voices screaming, *These teenagers need to take responsibility for what they have done. They need to be punished. Who do they think they are?* And so on and so on. But it is evident this is not working, and a better way must be found.

So once again, I quote from Bob Proctor's teachings. The American moral and social philosopher Eric Hoffer (1902 – 1983) observed: *'To a man utterly without a sense of belonging, mere life is all that matters. It is the only reality in an eternity of nothingness, and he clings to it with shameless despair.'*

I believe if everyone had a basic understanding of this concept of the conscious and subconscious mind, and if it could be taught all over the world, it would transform our world. Because this understanding and awareness transcends every race, every colour and every creed. It comes from the very heart of every mother and there is no greater love on earth than a mother's love for her child.

We are unique and we were born that way, so as unique human beings we have gifts that are special to us, but most of those who loved us and raised us had no idea who they, or we, really are; having a textbook way of raising a child but there are huge gaps missing.

This sort of thinking, understanding and awareness never came to me until after I was seventy years of age. I found it in a wonderful book called *Think and Grow Rich* by Napoleon Hill, first published way back in 1937.

He was quoting a wonderful English poet W E Henley who said: 'We are the masters of our fate and captains of our souls and the premise of this is because we can control our thoughts.'

It's amazing that we've had this knowledge for so long, but only now is it becoming mainstream.

Hill also said, 'Henley himself did not realise at the time, that the ether in which our little world floats in a form of energy and moves in a very high vibration, is filled with a universal power which adapts itself to the nature of our thoughts and transmutes our thoughts into their equivalent power.'

I will ask you once again my beautiful unique mums: *Do you know who you really are?*

You are a creator with this Infinite power I choose to call God and you need to understand that you are the co-creator manifesting this greater mystery on earth.

WHERE IS MY MUMMY?

But is it worth it? **You bet it is.**

Remember you are not alone on this journey, this creator walks with you on your incredible journey, as your baby is being knitted together in your marvellous womb. This creator who made heaven and earth and all of nature is always walking with you. All of the time.

CHAPTER 12
THE BURNT CHOP SYNDROME

Many times, we inadvertently bring about what we do not want, taking our frustrations out on others, blaming them for the plight we find ourselves in. Often, this is our family, those we love most.

I often hear women aggrieved over a situation where they feel they are being taken advantage of and they perceive their needs have not been considered or met. Although this may be difficult to hear or believe, but when this happens, women may have even brought it on themselves.

I have been guilty of this my whole life. I can still hear one of my daughter's say, 'Mum, you are choosing the "burnt chop again"?'

We have traditionally been seen as the homemaker and carers for our families. And whilst this is a role which can bring about the greatest joy in our life, we need to be very careful that what we think about, we bring about.

I see so many women cheat themselves of opportunities, be that in the world of academics, travel, social opportunities or very importantly taking time for themselves, as they are so busy taking care of their families, they end up denying themselves of so much in life.

The consequences come when they blame someone else for their missed opportunities and refuse to see it is them who has brought this about over many years. They didn't speak up, and in many of the situations, they didn't even question. They just went along giving the 'burnt chop syndrome' teeth, until one day they erupt, and their family just don't understand and may even consider them greedy.

Women often bring this on themselves when they consider themselves to be the one who waits on everybody else. Even the slogan on the family car *Mum's Taxi* contributes to this thinking. We willingly assume this position and even laugh about it, but in time, we end up blaming our loved ones for it.

We must remember to take care of ourselves. We should not expect others to look out for us. If they do, then we need to be grateful, but it should not be an expectation. We have a voice, USE IT.

I love the message in the movie *Shirley Valentine*, however, we do not need to come to reach this point in our lives if we have a great self-image and enough self-love within ourselves to navigate ourselves through life.

The movie *Shirley Valentine* was made in 1989. It resonated with so many of we women of that time because it mirrored to us how we had allowed ourselves to fall into what was coined *'the burnt chop syndrome'*. It was based on a forty-nine-year-old lady from Liverpool, England, who was married with two teenage children. She was forever at their beck and call, as well as that of her husband. One day she came to the point of throwing in the towel and when invited by a girlfriend to go on a holiday to Greece, she decided to go. After feeding the dog the steak dinner she had prepared for her husband on his return from work, she walked out and found a new way of living, which she enjoyed so much, she never went back.

The irony of this movie was that Shirley Valentine brought this situation on herself over many years by living 'the burnt chop syndrome'. Many of we women have been, or are in this same situation now, because we were not given the understanding and awareness of our own self-worth and self-love, or a healthy self-image.

No more excuses, no more using the blame game, it is time to take responsibility for our lives and make better choices for ourselves. This is the starting point for all of us. We need to understand *who we really are* and this begins by building a beautiful self-image, which will bring about a beautiful self-love; a self-love which nobody can destroy. As Sushil Aggarwal quoted on YouTube, *'When you know your worth no-one can make you feel worthless.'* This is your life, your one and only life, so make sure you make it your story.

Remember: Be careful how we speak to ourselves because *we* are *listening*.

This is so important for we mums to understand and pass onto our children.

THOUGHTS FOR MY CHILDREN AND GRANDCHILDREN

- Always follow your heart.
- Be true to yourself.

WHERE IS MY MUMMY?

- Life is a beautiful journey.
- Smile –it is easier than frowning.
- Laughter is the best medicine.
- Always think the best.
- Choose your friends carefully.
- Be a leader not a follower.
- You are enough.
- Deeds speak louder than words.
- Always look at the sunny side of life.
- Enjoy the success of others as you do your own.
- Follow your heart not the crowd.
- Always know the universe is on your side.
- Live your life with purpose.
- You are stronger than you think.
- Be patient and kind to yourself and others.
- Givers gain.
- Celebrate your *wins* and other people's as well.
- Respect your own and other people's boundaries.
- Remember your body belongs to you.
- Listen to others as you would have others listen to you.
- Be open-minded.
- Tell yourself you *love* yourself – every day.
- Know you are *loved* and always will be.
- Hug yourself every day.
- Create your own heaven on earth.

Now take a moment and walk a little journey with me.

How many times do we walk past a mirror at home or out shopping and look at ourselves and weigh up how we **see** ourselves – our weight, our choice of clothes etc. Sometimes in the positive, but I would tend to say more in the negative. But that being that, now I want to ask you, *Why do we do this over and over again, hardly passing a mirror without passing judgement good or bad on ourselves?*

Now a little exercise – tell me, how often do you stop to look at your face in a mirror and look into your eyes? No, not just when you are applying your mascara or eye shadow, I mean your eyes – yes, *your beautiful eyes.* It is a common expression believed by many that our eyes are the window of our soul. So how often do we look deep into our eyes?

We tend to say we look lovingly into the eyes of the one we love, that very special person in our life, however, I do not believe we do it to ourselves very often, if at all.

Strange, isn't it? So now how about we try it? Find a mirror in your home, bathroom, wardrobe, anywhere, just so long as you are in front of the mirror alone. Now centre in on your face and look into your eyes – one at a time is the best. Stand there thinking nothing and just *look* and *focus*. Now, when you feel you are focused, start talking to yourself. You might feel funny at first, but ignore this, as it is quite natural. And don't look over your shoulder, there is no-one there to hear you. Now start telling your inner child how much you love her, how beautiful she is and how safe she is with you. Slowly, slowly, slowly, focus deep within your eyes, one at a time. Time has stopped and you are all there is. If you continue, you will start to *feel* a sense of rapport with your inner child, a slow glow rising up in you, a vibration of love and joy. A smile will begin to creep across your face. This is one of the most beautiful healing and loving gifts anyone can give to themselves.

The feeling of love for this inner child comes to the fore and a sense of protection and comfort for this inner child starts to gather momentum within us. We have now started on a beautiful journey where we come to love ourselves more. If we continue over a period of *time,* we will start to find our inner child who has always been there. But there has been a lifetime of ignoring her and shutting her down. Whenever she has tried to surface, there has never been any time to connect with her, because we always thought the needs of others needed to be met first.

Or maybe you simply have never known or never been told you have an *inner being* who desperately needs your love.

Do not feel ashamed or unworthy, all the deeds of yesterday are forgotten. They are past and you cannot change anything. Except yourself.

Everything in life just *is,* so don't compare yourself to others. Comparing is robbing oneself of joy.

Today is a new day. We all have a past and for some of us, it is not pretty. We did things we wish we had not, however that is where it is … *in the past* … never to be thought of again. Walk on, walk on, with hope in your heart, for today is the first day of a beautiful new life. You really are enough *now*. Know it and accept it. Only *you* can do this.

Remember that today's accomplishments were yesterday's impossibilities.

CHAPTER 13
ATTITUDE

Attitude is a very interesting word. I had not paid much attention to it before, and then I heard someone say that **'it is the composite of our thoughts, feelings and actions'** (Earl Nightingale, 1966). As I took a closer look at this, it made sense. Because it is all about what we *think,* then what we *feel* and this leads into *action,* and of course, the *results* we see in our lives. Most often, we do not connect all these together and we wonder why we get the results we get.

Lao Tzu explains his way of understanding attitude as:
Watch your thoughts they become your words;
Watch your words they become your actions;
Watch your actions they become your habits;
Watch your habits they become your character;
Watch your character it becomes your destiny.

We come across people all throughout our lives, and some just have a lovely way of seeing things and thinking in a certain way; their company is such a nice place to be in. These people have a great attitude.

Others, we just want to steer clear of, as they complain, whinge and often have a victim mentality. Unless we are drawn to this sort of attitude resonating within us – and believe me, many of us do – we tend to want to steer clear. Remember the saying: *Birds of a feather flock together.* And this is so true.

Mahatma Gandhi understood this when he said: *'I will not allow dirty feet to walk through my mind.'*

Yes, Gandhi understood the sacredness of our minds and that we are the keeper of our minds. And we, being the guardians of our little ones, are responsible for the cleanliness of their minds until they can think for themselves. And then, they think from the richness and truth we have put into the treasures of their mind. What a responsibility!

Choose who you allow into your environment. Life is too short. Only allow those who have a great *attitude* to walk through your mind. This is so important as it is our attitude we pass onto our children.

A person with a great attitude is a person with great optimism. They always think the best will come out of any situation. A pessimistic person generally thinks in the negative.

This was so understood by the famous survivor of Auschwitz, Dr Viktor Frankl, who as they took his wedding ring from his hand, the last remnants of what was his visible world, he said, 'Our greatest freedom is the freedom to choose. You can take everything else from me but the one thing you cannot take away from me is the way I choose to respond to what you do to me. You can never make me think what I do not want to think.'

He understood that the most important gift we have, the last of one's freedoms is to choose one's attitude in any given circumstance. *Attitude* being how we **think, feel and act.**

Lou Holtz, a former football player and coach once said: 'Virtually nothing is impossible in this world if you just put your mind to it and maintain a positive attitude.'

I feel the need here to repeat this understanding of James Allen in his book *As a Man Thinketh:* 'Man is mind and evermore he takes the tool of thought and plants it as he wills. Brings forth a thousand joys, a thousand ills; he thinks in secret and it comes to pass. Environment is but his looking glass.'

… Because I believe James Allen understood what I did not see, could not see for quite some time, and what most of us may never be able to see, and that is: '… whatever we **think** becomes reality in our lives.'

Whatever we dwell on and think about, all day long, becomes who and what we are.

How true are these words? By the very proof of our existence, we all have been given a mind and our mind is our playground through which we shape our world, and this continues to be formed by our attitude.

A person who is optimistic always believes in a good outcome, the pessimist never tries, as he has an attitude that it probably won't work out and guess what 'he is probably right'. Best understood in these words from Henry Ford: 'Whether you think you can, or think you can't you're right.' How true is this?

Earl Nightingale, *Lead the Field* (1993), stated that: *'Attitude is a magic word, it creates awesome, wonderful things in our life.'*

Often our *attitude* shows up when we are in the company of others. It is here we see many people who have shown us a great attitude and they never allow circumstances to condition them. Rather, they take whatever circumstances come into their life and choose how they will respond to them. In other words, they condition their circumstances and never allow themselves to live in a victim mentality.

We are not born with an *attitude*; it is something we develop as we go through life, and it is our responsibility to instil a great *attitude* in our child from the word go. A great *attitude* will serve our child right through their life and it will open up doors of possibility to them, which might be considered by those with not so good an attitude, to be closed. It seems to me to be something rarely spoken of, whether through a lack of understanding or awareness, and yet so important for a happy and productive life.

Helen Keller is an incredible example. Becoming deaf and blind as a toddler, she added value to the lives of so many through educating others with disabilities, and especially advocating for women who were blind like herself, not allowing circumstance *to* rob her of her full potential.

Another one of our recent heroes was Stephen Hawking. When he was twenty-one years of age, he was diagnosed with early-onset motor neurone disease. Significantly, a person diagnosed with MND has a life expectancy of only two to three years. However, he did not allow this to stop him, as he had an incredible *attitude,* and he went on to revolutionise our understanding of the black hole in our universe which emits radiation and could be detected by special instrumentation. He lived until 2018, at which time he was seventy-six years old. Stephen Hawking continued to work all his life for the betterment of humankind.

Ludwig Van Beethoven, who gifted us the incredible Choral

Symphony No 9 was deaf. John Milton the great poet was blind, and someone we rarely hear about was Blair Hill, son of Napoleon Hill, who was the author of the infamous bestselling book *Think and Grow Rich*. Blair was born without any physical sign of ears and his parents were told at Blair's birth that he would be deaf and mute for life.

Blair was then diagnosed with bilateral microtia and, through the use of spinal manipulation, persistence and a desire to hear, he began his journey towards normal hearing.

When he was in his early twenties, Blair was offered a trial use of acousticon hearing aids which were made available to him by Dictograph Products Company, and he was able to hear perfectly. More importantly to him, it availed him of the way he could render useful service and give hope and practical relief to those who were deaf and would have been doomed forever to deaf mutism. A great *attitude* coupled with a desire to hear and incredible persistence contributed to the ability of Blair Hill to hear.

Beatrix Potter and J K Rowling both had their books rejected countless times, but through persistence and having a great attitude, pushed through and now their writings are history. Congratulations, **you did it. You made it happen.**

Another one of my champions is Sir Richard Branson, the founder of the Virgin group. In the 1970s, he was not born into wealth. He had dyslexia and produced a poor academic performance. It has been reported that on his last day at school, his headmaster told him he would either end up in prison or become a millionaire. I admire him because he did not come through the regular university roads but would turn his hand to anything if it looked like a reasonable opportunity. He had vision, and with the right *attitude,* coupled with persistence and desire, he has added much value to the lives of so many people all over the world.

Many other people in the field of sports, politics, philosophy, science and those in our everyday communities have contributed to the beautiful life we live today. They encourage us to keep going when things seem tough, or even when things seem unfair, because a healthy attitude shows us that nothing is impossible.

Each of these examples I have researched myself through books, podcasts, movies and the wonderful gift of Google search. They inspire us and enhance our gratitude for the lives we ourselves have the potential to live today.

Each one of us can add value to people every day, in our own special way, through a smile, a positive response or a word of encouragement. One never knows what ripples we cause to happen when we step out with a great attitude.

Attitude mixed with faith and desire is what ran through the minds of these amazing people who added such value to the lives of many people.

And for me 'faith' is best understood in the words of Clarence Smithison, in the wonderful book *You Were Born Rich* by Bob Proctor: *'Faith is the ability to see the invisible, believe in the incredible and receive what the masses believe to be impossible.'*

A *faith-filled person* is said to be one who goes through life with their cup *half-full,* whereas a person who is pessimistic is said to see life with their cup *half-empty.*

CHAPTER 14
TIME

I have never heard anyone on their deathbed say they wished they had more money. They say it or think it almost every day of their lives but on their deathbed the only thing they really want more of, is *time*. I myself, wish I had my time again to do the things that really mattered that I never found the time to do. Or if I had my time again, I would spend it differently.

Rather their regret is for the things they have done or have not done, or the things they would do differently. *Time* to spend just one more day with their loved ones. *Time* is what we all want.

Time waits for no man. You cannot store it up in a bank account for another day in the future; for once it has passed it has gone forever. Even retirement. Many people will say, *I can't wait until I retire,* or as one person said to me on his birthday recently, when I wished him a Happy Birthday, he said, *One more birthday gone before I retire.* So, I asked him, *And what does retirement mean to you?* And his reply was, *Just hanging around.*

In other words, *time* is what he was looking forward to. How sad to look forward to a time that may not ever come.

WHERE IS MY MUMMY?

Time is for now. There are no guarantees for the future, not even for the end of this day or end of this hour or minute. *Time* goes merrily on its way.

In Bob Proctor's lectures in *The Success Puzzle,* Earl Nightingale suggests that: 'No-one manages "time", we only manage activities.'

Nature displays this to us in all its incredible ways. Just like all the universe, the tides go in and the tides go out, the sun rises and sets, and even though we try to manipulate this thing called *time* as we change our clocks, we are only managing our activities, we are not managing time, as the sun will keep coming up and going down each day. *Time* is its own master, and so, it is up to us to manage our activities wisely and enjoy the *time* we have. We all have the same time in our life, there are twenty-four hours in one day and it is totally up to us how we use it. Nobody will judge us on how we spend it, but the evidence will always be there in our results.

Remember, one day you will wake up and discover there is no more time to do the things you dreamed of.

I heard the song 'Cats in the Cradle' by Harry Chapin, way back in 1974 when my son was four years old. It touched me then and I think it is worth including this in my story for it really does put these words into reality. I recommend you Google the lyrics, as its meaning is profound.

Our time is the most precious gift we can give a child, and when the time is gone it is gone forever. Yes, the intention was always there, however it was never translated into time spent with those we love.

It just passes through our hands like the sand through an hourglass, ever so quietly, ever so smoothly; it was here and now it is gone.

And *time* is the most important thing we can give our child.

An hourglass can explain this so simply. The sand in the bottom is gone forever – that was yesterday's *time*. The sand in the top is the *time of tomorrow* and there are no guarantees of that. We don't even know if we will be here tomorrow, or next month, or next year; there are no guarantees. However, we do have the sand in the middle and that represents *now*. That is the only time we are certain of – **time now.**

Neither the past nor the future is important. The past is gone. The future is not guaranteed. *Now* it the only *time* we have. Use your time wisely; make memories. It really is the little things that count. Be at peace and be grateful, no matter what. Always choose the good side of life.

CHAPTER 15
SLEEP

I was told when I was growing up that the 'eight-hour day' was something past generations had fought hard for; something we today should be forever grateful for. This thinking of an eight-hour day came about by a social movement on 21 April 1856, when stonemasons downed tools and walked off the job in protests over their employer's refusal to accept their demands for reduced working hours. This brought employers to the negotiating table and led to an agreement, whereby stonemasons worked no more than eight hours a day and it enshrined the philosophy of how important it was to have sleep, rest and play. Eight hours for each within a twenty-four-hour period.

I believe very few people have an understanding of the most productive and therefore most important eight-hour period within this philosophy, as they think of all the *play* they can have and that is so good. True, play with the family, sharing a family meal, relaxing and spending time with friends is all very important, however, it may come as a shock to be awakened to the notion of *sleep* being one of the most productive times in a person's day.

How is this possible? one would ask. One would be inclined to believe that **work** was the most logical.

This is because very few people understand how necessary and valuable *sleep* is, and what actually happens when we go to sleep.

So, do you know what happens when we go to sleep? As we drift into sleep and slip into a semi-conscious state, our conscious mind goes to sleep, however, our subconscious mind remains wide open, as it never sleeps.

The thoughts we entertain directly before we drop off to sleep become our plaything for the eight hours of our sleep time, be it positive or negative. That is why it is unwise to fill one's mind with disturbing thoughts and pictures before we retire to sleep, because we continue to replay these images throughout our eight-hour sleep time.

It can be viewed like the story we all know from our childhood, *Aladdin and His Magic Lamp*. We can choose what we really want and visualise it in our powerful beautiful minds as we drop off to sleep. Yes, feed our wishes, desires and magical, powerful thoughts into our minds. And then to cap it all off, let it be the first thought in our minds upon awakening.

Once again, become emotionally involved with this visualisation as you drop off to sleep, and use vibration to get yourself into a beautiful place. Vibration is brought about by *how we feel*. Thinking beautiful thoughts that bring us into a lovely place. It is how we feel, and in the morning as you come out of your sleep, think of what you were visualising when you drifted off to sleep the night before. Powerful stuff.

The understanding being that, when we sleep, the conscious

subjective (thinking mind) shuts down, and the subconscious deductive (emotional mind) stays wide awake. And remember, the subconscious mind is deductive, it cannot differentiate between what is real and what is unreal. Therefore, we can feed it a lie and it will accept it, as it doesn't care, it has no ability to reject. So, use your powerful, wonderful imagination to conjure up what you really desire for your life.

This is one of the most exciting, liberating and enlightening understandings I have ever come to learn.

This may even have some bearing on why we can wake up more tired than when we went to sleep, because we engage with what was going on in our minds before we dropped off to sleep.

We could have been wrestling a giant tiger in Africa in the movie we just saw. Or re-enacting the torture of our negative bank balance sheet, having spent the previous hour before bedtime going over the negative financial reviews. We could have been the main character in a murder-mystery novel we were reading before we dropped off to sleep.

That is why we are always advised to turn off the television, or our other devices, half an hour before we retire and listen to some soothing meditative music, or just lie there and relax. Anything that will settle us down and prepare us for the eight hours ahead.

Sleep has become my favourite friend, but remember everything works in harmony and the eight-hour work rest and play thinking is important, as they all have their own energies.

Sleep is especially important to our little ones, since they grow as they sleep. It is generally accepted that we continue to grow physically until our late teens or early twenties, and this is thought to be controlled primarily by the growth hormone made in the pituitary gland.

There are those who use this magical time to sort out their problems. By using this time to program into their subconscious whatever solutions they are looking for, and then slip into their eight-hour playground.

I did this many times when I was going through university, at the ripe old age of fifty-three. I would go to sleep with a thought in my mind of a paper I was working on, one I just couldn't seem to get right in my waking hours. I just couldn't find the right words, and often I would wake up in the middle of the night and scribble down the exact words or solution on a piece of paper that had come to me in my dreams, and then fall straight back to sleep. Next morning, I would wake refreshed with the answer to my question right before my eyes. I still use this practice today and regard my 'sleep' TIME as my most creative and effortless time spent on a problem. I ask for the solution and rarely am I disappointed.

That is precisely why it is so important *what* we feed our little ones, as they fall off to sleep. I am so aware of the damage that negative violent behaviours are now feeding into the minds of our teenagers, as they choose to use their phones as their 'storyteller' as they drift off to sleep, feeding this negative material into their precious open and receptive minds.

On the flipside, many teenagers can also use this sleep opportunity as their most productive time if feeding their subconscious mind with the positive images that will improve their lives. It comes down to being aware of this working of our mind and then *choose* to work with it.

Yes, *choose* what we do with our sleep time, it really is up to us.

WHERE IS MY MUMMY?

We all have the same time and it's about what we choose to do with it. Always remember, we are the master of our minds, for the good or the negative.

CHAPTER 16
GRATITUDE

We teach our children to say *thank you* and this is regarded as good manners. It is lovely to hear someone say *thank you* for services rendered, whether this is to the person on the check-out for our groceries, the chappie at the petrol station, when we receive a gift or for the service we receive in a restaurant. However, whilst saying thank you is part of it, gratitude is so much more.

Gratitude comes from the *heart*. It is an emotional response; it is a feeling. It goes beyond just the words *thank you* and leaves a profound effect.

Train your heart and mind to see beauty in everything. There is always something to be grateful for.

This also happens when we change our perception of things, for if we choose only to look at the positive or good in a situation, generally, we are happier, some would say, *Take off your rose-coloured glasses*, but I would say, WHY?

Allow your children to keep their rose-coloured glasses on and always look at the brighter side of life. Do not rob them of their childlike simplicity, their dreaming their joy. Build their dreams and enter into them with them, it is pure magic.

Gratitude opens one's heart and lets the sunshine in. It is as if a light has been turned on in our lives. When we tuck our little ones into bed, sit with them and teach them to be **_grateful_**. Grateful for the little things in life. Their family, their friends, the food they eat the clothes they wear, the air they breathe, nature all around them and the roof over their head. Yes, teach them to be grateful.

We as family, at times, would choose to go around the dinner table and listen as each person shares something they are grateful for that day. It is beautiful how a sense of harmony and peace permeates those present. We also get an insight into the day of our loved ones. This allows our children to share something that many grown-ups have no confidence in doing. Yes, gratitude has so many benefits.

Develop an *attitude of gratitude* and it will be your best friend. It will walk with you all the days of your life. It is a feeling that brings with it peace, love and joy. Teach it to your child and you will have gifted them one of the most precious gifts they could ever receive.

Gratitude is my *'morning elixir'*. No matter how I may be feeling, after I spend ten minutes writing out a few things I'm grateful for, I always come into my 'happy place' and I feel a smile growing on my face. It is the most beautiful feeling. Yes, it truly is my 'morning elixir'. Trust me and try it.

Today, it is quite common to find people who choose to write out a list of what they are grateful for each morning. This may include gratitude for family, health or something special that has happened to them in their daily life. I always say anything that brings a smile to my face brings gratitude. Remember, it is a *'feeling'*.

Treat yourself to a little journal. Have fun choosing the perfect one for you, full of blank pages where you will be the author. Each morning, rise a wee bit early, enough time to grab a cup of coffee, sit in your favourite chair in a quiet place all by yourself and begin to write. You may have to rise a little earlier than normal, but you alone can make this choice. Remember this is your time; it belongs to nobody else.

Begin to write three things you are grateful for. There is no right or wrong way to write, whatever pops into your mind. Some find this the most difficult part, just to start, because they have never really stopped and expressed gratitude like this before.

I promise you that in doing this practice of gratitude more and more, things will start to flow from your pen.

It is not important if you write three or thirty-three, it is the gratitude you *feel* that is important, the feeling that will start to well up from within you and the peace and joy you feel. Yes, this is what is the most important. It is the vibration that one comes into when gratitude fills your heart. You will know it when you feel it.

When you make this a habit in your life, it really can change the way you look at things, your perception, and as we now know, as we change the way we look at things, those things change.

CHAPTER 17
PRAISE

Children will glow with happiness and joy; they will literally beam when they receive *praise*. Their smiles will stretch from ear to ear; it is so beautiful to see.

Praise is one of the most beautiful gifts one can give to another human being. Given sincerely and freely, it can change the vibration in the air around us. More than the medal around one's neck, *praise* is sought by us from our fellow human beings. How often do we read the acclamation or recognition on a Facebook post for some achievement, we or our loved ones have received, whether it be in the field of sport, academia or in the attainment of a new job or in the field of movies or the arts? Yes, even we enjoy the receiving of praise. Given with a generous heart, it can be so powerful, it can literally change lives.

Our little ones look for and receive *praise* for their early accomplishments in life, however, we often slowly and unknowingly stop giving them praise. Maybe it is because we were brought up with the notion that you will spoil the child. Often, we can even go further and tell them: *Now don't you get too big for your boots,* or, *You got a B, why didn't you get an A*, or, *Now you have done that, I will expect it all the time.*

I have never believed anyone can *spoil* a child if we are acting out of love. However, if praise is withheld, we may kill the feeling of self-worth and self-image within our child.

Meekness was drummed into us as children, but it was so misunderstood. True meekness is knowing who we truly are and responding to our fellow human beings in the same vein. This applies to our life within the home, in the playground, at day care, in the shopping centre and in the workplace. Yes, it is the yardstick of our true selves. Teach it to your children by the example you show. Meekness will then journey with them all the days of their lives.

Praise children, praise their self-esteem and watch them ***grow***.

This is what we hungered for in ourselves as children. We know that *feeling*. We remember that feeling when we were young and when it never came. It affected our self-esteem and feeling of self-worth. *Now* remember to use *words*. Praise your child *now*, for the little everyday things they do. When we verbally praise our children, their bodies vibrate – yes, they actually do. They vibrate, we all do. Praise children whether they do well or not, in anything they do. Always build up their self-confidence, self-love and, ultimately, their self-image.

Praise opens a door in their minds and makes our child want to do better. Take for example a sniffer dog at the airport. When given a treat for sniffing out illegal substances, they feel really good about themselves. If this works for a dog, imagine what it does for a child. We always need to remember that condemnation closes their heart, while praise opens their heart.

WHERE IS MY MUMMY?

I have heard it said that when in the presence of the Dalai Lama, there is a radiance that surrounds the whole audience. They call it *thought transference.* The positive vibes the Dalai Lama gives off affects every person in the room.

Way back in 1939, Semyon and Valentina Kirlian, a Russian couple, discovered the aura that can be seen surrounding people when a photo was taken in a certain light. It was known as the Kirlian Photography.

We really are glistening vibrating bodies, we just don't have the awareness to be able to see it.

We can so often seek the negative in others; but rather we need to always look for the good, the accomplishments of others and praise them, be it a child or an adult, it works the same.

I love this poem, *If I Knew You,* by Nixon Waterman. It really speaks of the truth of understanding one another:

If I knew you and you knew me
If both of us could clearly see.
And with an inner light divine
The meaning of your heart and mine.

I'm sure that we would differ less
And clasp our hands in friendliness
Our thoughts would pleasantly agree,
If I knew you and you knew me.

It may well stretch us because our way of pulling people down and finding fault is so impregnated in our society, and it takes courage to stop ourselves in our tracks and refrain from pulling people down, which nearly always happens when the person spoken about is not present

A friend of mine gave me this way of thinking: *Never say anything about a person unless you would want them in the room with you to hear it.* Look only for the good in everyone and we will be happier people.

However, it starts with us. Look only for the good and we all will be happier and walk around with a smile on our face. I would like to leave you with this wonderful insight into how our *thinking* works. It is a poem by Henry Van Dyke:

Thoughts Are Things

I hold it true that thoughts are things;
They're endowed with bodies and breath and wings.
And that we send them forth to fill
The world with good results or ill.
That which we call our secret thought
Speeds forth to earth's remotest spot,
Leaving its blessings or its woes
Like tracks behind it as it goes.

We build our future, thought by thought,
For good or ill, yet know it not.
Yet so the universe was wrought.
Thought is another name for fate;
Choose thy destiny and wait,
For love brings love and hate brings hate.

CHAPTER 18
NON-RESISTANCE

I include this in this book because I have found it to be of such value in my life. It has been a 'change-breaker' for me. The word itself *non-resistance* can conjure up different thoughts and, may I say, reactions, because it is so misunderstood.

I believe that if every person understood what this is, and how to use it, we would live in a world of non-violence, a world of harmony. This is so very important for our teenagers, where violence plays such a big part in their environment.

When one hears the word resistance, one tends to see a blockage, a wall, something they need to break through or bring down, and this entails effort and hard work. So, non-resistance is being the opposite. It brings a feeling of release, peace and harmony.

One might think this is just copping out or giving in, however, this is not what non-resistance means.

When I choose to react, I am giving away my power, yet when I respond, I am staying in control of myself. Non-resistance is choosing to *respond* rather than to *react*. Remember, reacting is a habit. By responding one has to think.

This was one of the most difficult understandings I had to work through, for 'confrontation' was the way we dealt with issues in our family. It was considered a healthy, strong and necessary way to communicate. We were a family who thrived on 'confrontation' and we would not let a difference of opinion go. It makes me tired thinking of it now, and the energy that was wasted was deplorable.

I started to get an insight into this over the last few years, and realised how tired I was of all the confrontation. However, I found it was not easy to change the way I reacted, as people 'expected' me to be confrontational as this is the person I had always shown up to be. But I was getting tired of it and saw the damage it was doing in my life, making the decision to let it go and not to argue.

Rather than seeing myself as docile and an easy target, I became the one in charge. I became peaceful, happy and loving, and started to live in harmony with people. It has been truly liberating.

I could still see the issues, but I chose to only respond and never react. This took the heat, the wasted energy out of the argument, and I thus, gave no more ammunition to the situation. People often said *I was now boring*, but I knew I was no longer feeding their energy, and so, retained my own energy.

Teach our little ones a better way – to *respond* rather than to *react*. Be an example first in your own life and then teach them through their situations with others.

Truly, it will be the most liberating skill you can teach your child. Using nature as an example, teach them how a mighty river starts off as a little stream high up in the mountains. It starts off as a trickle, with no ability to push over the big boulders or branches that block its way, but the little stream will find a way around, over and under these obstacles, as it marches its way down the hillside, forever on its mission. It gains volume and strength, as it continues on, until eventually it flows into the mighty river. The boulders and branches could have been obstacles, but it chose to move around and over them and just go quietly on its way, steadily and with no purpose other than to reach its destination.

There was nothing *weak* about this stream; but it did not waste its time or energy demanding its right of way. We need to teach our children this same strategy as a little one, so they are mighty in mind and understanding when they encounter these boulders and obstacles in their life. Responding rather than reacting. Oh, what a better world we would live in. A world of peace and harmony.

This choice favours *you* as it takes away the malice, anger and arguments which sap our energy and the control which comes into play when one reacts. If we have a relaxed attitude, the energy will just flow.

Anytime we talk about unfavourable conditions or situations that seem *unfair,* we create resistance to what we want. Watch people in the shopping malls when someone thinks they have been overlooked or someone pushed in, and especially when looking for a parking spot at the shopping centre. It does become very obvious, and one can see the tension, anger and lack of control that comes into play.

Take notice in a restaurant when someone is not happy about the service or their meals. The way one approaches the situation will tell you so much about *who they are* and from which angle they are coming from. One of response or one of reaction, which is generally seen to be taken personally. The waste of human energy is appalling. We cannot change anything on the outside, but we can choose to change how we respond from the inside.

If a person resists a situation, he will have it with him. The person who uses non-resistance is not weak; he is strong as he allows it to pass by. When you agree with your enemy, it disarms him. There is nothing to argue about. Over time, the one who is your adversary will become your friend. You are the winner when you refuse to argue.

Abraham Lincoln, a past President of the United States, had this beautiful understanding of non-resistance. It was once said that when he was choosing his cabinet he was asked why he appointed ministers who were always opposing him. His response was, 'When I have made them my friends, haven't I destroyed my enemies?' Such a beautiful understanding of non-resistance.

Branch Rickey was an American baseball player who coached the Brooklyn Dodgers. He said one time that he didn't care how well a person could hit the ball, how fast they could run, how well they could throw the ball; but if they weren't as loose as ashes he wouldn't hire them. He was looking for that magic word *harmony* in his team. Guys who could play *together*. Play as a *team*. Those who would put the game before their own personal gain.

Yes, it is so true, you are the *winner* when you refuse to argue.

Meekness is the strength appropriated when we do not argue, when we do not become angry and boastful and proud, when we do not insist upon having our rights in a quarrelsome manner.

'Meekness is the steel of one's nature. It is enduring, it is the strength that you win an argument by refusing to argue.' Working with the Law ~ Raymomd Holliwell

CHAPTER 19
SACRIFICE

When we think of 'sacrifice', we tend to think of something we are being asked to give up, and it often entails giving up something we enjoy or treasure.

However, whilst we are called to give up *something*, it is the giving up of something of a 'lower nature' in our lives for something of 'higher nature'.

Take for example when we want to 'release' weight (I use the word *release* rather than *lose* because when one *loses* something psychologically one tends to 'find it again'. However, when one *releases* something, it is gone, never to return) and start to *choose* healthier foods versus unhealthy foods, and start to exercise rather than sit on the coach and watch TV, then we are giving up a lesser thing for a *higher* thing.

It's the same as overspending on purchases we don't really need and deciding to use this money more wisely, for example: saving for a holiday, a home or anything that adds value to our lives and the lives of others.

Deciding to turn off the telly and find something more creative to do – gardening, walking, community activities or reading – yes, using our 'time' more productively.

It is a beautiful concept, and if you have not thought of it this way before, it's a rewarding way to live.

Teaching our children in their early years to understand and use *sacrifice* as a positive in their life is such an amazing tool that will benefit them throughout their lives.

Once in place and understood, it can be the most freeing and satisfying tool we could ever have in our kit.

We can start this understanding even with our children at a tender age, with their choice of food, giving up the unhealthy choices for more nourishing and healthy foods. I remember my two young grandsons were always presented with a plate of attractive fruits for morning tea rather than biscuits and cake. Now, in their early adulthood, they have healthy, happy eating habits. Yes, it has certainly paid off.

If our children are taught this as a little ones, then when they are teenagers and have the pressure of their mates egging them on to take risks or take drugs for an instant gratification, then by choosing to use this understanding of *sacrifice,* they will continue to gain a higher reward by the continuous use and pleasure of the freedom of driving and having a healthy happy body.

I know when I decided to limit my drinking habits, I did so as I was realising that after a couple of drinks, I was not able to add good value to any conversation going on around me, and I was disappointed later when I wished I could have felt more cognitive. I discovered the enjoyment of being able to contribute more to the conversation around me.

Having made this decision, I now enjoy conversing with my

friends and family so much more and look forward to enjoying and remembering the conversations that result.

Yes, a small sacrifice, but has it been worth it. Absolutely.

We did not always create these unhealthy habits in our lives, but it is we, as adults, who now have the responsibility of changing them for a happier and healthier life.

Now, wouldn't it be better to give our little ones good habits to send them on their way? Take neatness in their life. This will save them time, as they will be able to find what they want when they want it and give them more time for pleasure. This is important for our little ones as they transition to school studies. By implementing good habits early in their life, it will gain them much more in time, enjoyment and self-discipline, producing less stress in their lives.

Nature is a great teacher, and if we look at her methods, we can see them in action and use their wisdom in our lives. The lesson here is to understand the power at work. If you just consider water flow, for example, if it is allowed to flow everywhere its power is not used, but if you harness the power, say in a turbine, you can use it to generate more power.

We can see evidence of this everywhere around us. It can be seen in our elite sportspeople who rise very early in the morning to practice, practice and practice some more. They give up their warm comfy bed to achieve something of a higher nature. The same for students wishing to attain a higher standard in their future life by attending university or doing a trade so they will have a higher income for their future. They sacrifice the money they can earn now for a higher qualification that may lead to more money in their later life.

Lastly, I will share an experience I had which drove home to me this idea of *sacrifice* working as a law in our life.

It was when I first started watching the game of softball. There is a principle used when playing softball, that when I first saw it played, I could not grasp it as it seemed so illogical to me. It was not until I saw the reasoning behind it that I understood the true nature behind the move.

It happens when a person *sacrifices* themselves by hitting what is called a 'bunt' and this will most likely get them 'out' because they are almost certain to get run out before they reach first base, and that is normally what the game is all about, getting to the first, second and third bases and then *home*, which scores a runner a point for their team. However, if there is a player on the third base who has an opportunity to get home and score a point for the team, the batter on the diamond is willing to *sacrifice* himself to get the person on third base 'home' then that is the *sacrifice* the batter has made for his team.

The batter sacrificed himself, and that sounds 'illogical', but if reasoned out, the aim of the game is to get the most runners home for their team.

It took me a long time to understand this, but the winner is not always the one who gets the glory but the one *'who brings the team home'*.

Reasoning is not always 'to the best and fastest' but in bringing out the best for everyone.

CHAPTER 20
FORGIVENESS

Forgiveness is probably one of the most misunderstood concepts in our world today. One hears so often the words, *I will never forgive him for what he did*. This is so very sad, for true forgiveness brings us freedom and it is not necessarily intended to bring freedom to others. If we choose not to *forgive*, we are keeping ourselves in a prison.

Think about it. You have a perceived wrong done against you and you think by using forgiveness, this allows the wrong doer to win; however, this is not necessarily true. The one who forgives is set *free* by this forgiving. I had a situation many years ago in which I asked a lady if she could mind my children for a few hours one night, as I had done this for her many times in the past. She said no and went on her merry way, not giving another thought to it. As for me, I seethed on it for years – yes, years, asking myself, *How could she say no?* It robbed me of my peace for so long, and it was not until I came to understand what real forgiveness was all about, that I could set myself free. And what's more, it works in every situation; in small situations like this, to the most horrendous situations in our lives. It never changes and it is available to everyone.

Forgiveness by me frees *me;* the other person may never ever know of it, and it is not even necessary for them to know, as I have within me the ability to choose whether I want to be free or not. We are not giving up anything, we are *gaining* by forgiving. We are gaining peace, joy and happiness, otherwise we will remain angry, resentful, hurt and unhappy. And this will forever control us. We are allowing the other person *control of us* by *how we feel*. As I said, this non-forgiving and resentment kept me in bondage for many years.

Religion really did try to teach us this, but somehow for me, I must not have had my listening ears turned on, or maybe religion didn't know how to express it in a way that people could see 'forgiveness' in the beautiful concept of true *freedom*.

I remember so well as a young girl, the law in my church was that one must go to confession the night before mass (usually Saturday) and confess any sins or grievances, etc. before Sunday mass and taking Communion. Mind you, one did know that all eyes would be on you if you did not front up for Communion, as they knew something was not right. The understanding behind this was that confession brought us into forgiveness and therefore freedom.

The concept itself was right, however, it never taught us that, we ourselves, have that same power to forgive and set ourselves free. Really it is quite self-serving, because we gain every time. I hope the one who I perceived has hurt me received a degree of freedom also, however, this is not my responsibility, they also need to forgive or ask for forgiveness of themselves if they have any residue of hurt from the situation and wish to be free.

Such a very important understanding and we need to teach our children, from a very young age, that *forgiveness* is something we do for and by ourselves; we never leave it in the control of another person. **Forgiveness is freedom.** How beautiful is that?

Forgiveness is to *let go completely*. Totally abandon the grudge, unforgiveness, hurt, resentment, anger and totally let go.

Forgiveness is a shift in perception that removes a block in *me*. If I choose not to forgive it remains a blockage in me, whilst the other person waltzes off happily into the never-never.

Sounds unfair, doesn't it? However, when properly understood, it is the greatest doorway to freedom one could ever walk through.

And the good news is the ball is in my court. Imagine if I was relying on the other person to forgive me and I could not be set free until they did.

Forgiving yourself and letting go of the guilt, or unforgiveness, is such a beautiful and healthy thing. It is like a medicine as it removes blockages in our life.

Forgiveness is limitless and the more we do it the easier it gets as we see the benefits are all ours. It is almost 'selfish and self-centred', because it really is something that benefits me, when sometimes the other person is totally oblivious to it.

This *understanding* has always been there, it just lacked the *conscious awareness*.

The real question is: *Am I willing to become the person I need to be to raise this child who has been entrusted to me, and in the process become a happier, more loving and peaceful person myself?*

Forgiveness not properly understood will keep you bound forever; you can never be free. Do not be deluded into thinking it is *getting you off the hook* and therefore you have escaped punishment. You have always been free, but it has been your unwillingness to accept forgiveness from yourself that has been the issue.

Chapter 21
WHO AM I?

Now we come to this question again: *Who am I?* and, *Why am I here?*

Who am I: When you truly can say, 'I know, that I know, that I know who I really am', nothing and no-one can take away your understanding and awareness of who you really are. For this realisation does not come from your head but from deep within your heart. You are unique and you are all-powerful. There is nobody quite like you and you have been created in the likeness and image of your God. Never forget that.

You are a co-creator with this infinite power and you are the co-creator manifesting the greatest mystery on Earth. The creation of what is the most marvellous incredible creation, in all this vast universe – a *unique perfect human being*, never to have been created before, for every human being is totally unique. Just as there are no two snowflakes quite the same, there is no-one ever created just like **you** and there is nobody created like this beautiful human being you have formed within your womb. Congratulations, *you* are a ***mum***.

NOW, WHY AM I HERE?

For those of you who have chosen to take this journey, you may well be asking yourself, *Is it all worth it?* All the tiredness, all the changes to your body forever, all the decision-making, energy-sapping commitments that call on every ounce of your mind, body and spirit, each and every day forever; my resounding answer is **yes**.

It blows my mind when I think of all that has been in operation, in our background for centuries, through our genetic history, to form each one of us. Our personal biological composition, the environment that has fashioned and moulded us into the person we are today and *now*, as we stand at the threshold of once again creating another incredible amazing human being, unique in every way. And *we*, yes, *we* are the *mummy*, the *co-creator*, of this tiny human being placed in our hands to bring out all that is already within them.

All the power, potential, awareness, understanding, ability, imagination, reasoning and will. Yes, everything is within this tiny little baby just waiting for us – their *mummy* – to draw it out of them, so as to become all that they were meant to be.

The good news is you do not walk alone; your God walks with you. Literally call on this infinite spirit in times of need and it will be there to guide you. You really never, ever walk alone.

Now I have been brought to this one last question.

WHAT IS MY PURPOSE?

I now understand who I am and why I am here, but there is still one lingering question I need to answer: *What is my purpose?*

And then came the *answer*: I am here to create *a* **legacy**

CHAPTER 22
LEGACY

I believe everyone holds a dream – a purpose in their life. And this dream, this purpose, belongs only to them. In the words of Earl Nightingale in his book, *The Leading Edge*: 'This great dream this surging dynamic thing invisible to all the world except to the person who holds it is responsible for every great advance of human life.'

When one hears the word *legacy*, most immediately think of inheritance, however, inheritance is then often conceptualised in monetary terms. Remember, it is not in what you *get* but in what you ARE. Everything you have at the time of your death belongs to someone else. **But what you are will last forever.**

One such legacy I would like to share came about with no understanding of it from me at the time.

In 1995, my husband and I purchased a two-acre rural property at Caboolture, an hour north of Brisbane, Queensland, Australia.

We never intended to live on it but bought it as an investment property for our daughter to live on with her horses and dogs, having just finished her teaching degree and been offered a position at the local high school.

Nine years later, we chose to retire to the property ourselves, and over the next seventeen years we created a magnificent garden and a playground for our seven grandchildren. We created many beautiful memories for our children and grandchildren, including a nine-hole golf course, cricket pitch, AFL posts, beautiful riding tracks and much serenity with peaceful nooks and crannies around the dam.

For me, the creation of the garden with dozens of trees, a two-hundred-metre long pathway, which meandered through the gardens and the serenity of a lotus pond where one could sit and be still, was etched on my heart and I always imagined it would be a place where people could come and find happiness, peace and joy.

We decided to move in 2021, as the management of the property was becoming too much and was affecting our health. Unbeknownst to us, the new buyer was intending to carve up the property for sixteen town houses, stripping all this beautifully created garden of its peace and serenity. However, there were more powerful forces at work, and it was revealed that the local council had earmarked our property for a local playground.

This is the legacy I speak about now, and it is much more than just a garden, it is a concept that reaches far and wide into the next generation and all the generations to come, not only to my immediate family, but a gift for all; to those who I may never get to meet. Now all children can come and enjoy what we created, and mothers can sit and soak up the peace and serenity of the lotus pool and the beautiful trees that now have a haven to grow and thrive. This is a very special *legacy* I leave to my family.

WHERE IS MY MUMMY?

Legacy is like air in my lungs. It motivates me. It moves me. It inspires me to get up in the morning and get going. My garden called for everything in me at the time and I am so happy and grateful for the idea that used me. However, the pages of *this book* have lain on my heart for many years now, ever since I heard those words, *Where is My Mummy?*

Those few words wrapped themselves around my heart, and I knew the day would come when they would have to be answered.

I am a mother. I am a grandmother; and my heart is drawn to the teenagers of today because I know it is **we**, their **mothers,** who hold their futures in our hands.

I have raised my children and seven grandchildren who are now all exiting their teenage years, and I now know I can no longer sit on what I have come to know, because many of our beautiful teenagers are slowly losing their way and many may not find their way back. Then one day we will wake up and it may be too late.

I speak of this book as a *legacy* for all women to the furthest ends of the earth, so they will truly understand *who they really are* and the power that is *within them*, as they impact the generations of the future to run faster, jump higher, dream bigger, always reaching for more ways to expand and fully express their God-given talents that they were endowed with at conception – for themselves, their families and the greater world. Their world. This is my dream my purpose and now a legacy for all women, for all mums.

Within all we women – and I say **all women** – for this understanding and awareness resonates within *all we women* all over the world. *Yes, all we women,* as each one of us are connected. Within us is all the wisdom, understanding, knowledge, fortitude and love to change this planet, which we are all part of and responsible for. Equipped with these wonderful tools we have now become aware of, and knowing the truth of *who we really are* and *who our child really is* 'an *infinite powerful force*'. We can now move forward using our powerful conscious and subconscious minds which have the power to melt, mould and guide us and our precious little ones of today through our – and their – marvellous life.

We have an understanding of how it is of the uttermost importance to build healthy and happy *self-love, self-belief* and ultimately a beautiful *self-image* of ourselves. One that nobody can ever destroy.

We also now have the *awareness* and *understanding* of these wonderful life-changing tools of attitude, gratitude, praise, non-resistance, forgiveness and sacrifice and we can take advantage of the wonderful understanding of sleep and time management and use them to make our dreams come true, teaching our little ones to do the same.

Yes, *legacy* is what you *give* of yourself to those you love. We give our time, our energy, our wisdom, our money and our love, and now we can *give* to those we love an *understanding* and *awareness* of our marvellous minds. We can only *give* what is within us. Some legacies we can only create in our hearts and their evolution will come about in due time. It is all about *giving*.

Know that our greatest *legacy* is who we are.

In the marvellous words of James Allen, *As a Man Thinketh* (1903): 'Lift our heads up high. Open our eyes wide and wake up and know that in the ocean of life the isles of blessedness are smiling and the sunny shore of our ideal awaits our coming.

Keep our hands firmly upon the helm of thought. In the core

of our soul reclines the commanding master. He does but sleep. Wake Him. Self-control is strength. Right thought is mastery. Calmness is power.'

We are the spirit who resides within. We are the commanding master. *now*, with this awareness and understanding we now know we have all we need within us to nurture and guide the greatest and the most incredible creation in all the marvellous universe – *a human being*. Not only physically but in the fullness of mind, body and spirit. We truly have everything within us *now*.

'God's gift to me is more talent, more ability than I could ever use in my lifetime and my gift to God is to use this talent and ability and become the person I was created to be.' – Steve Bow.

Our legacy is to add value to this world in everything we say and do, and to be the educator of the most precious human beings in *our* world today, our children and our teenagers of today and who are our leaders of the future.

This is our legacy. For every woman, every mother to know, 'who they are' and 'why they are here.'

Golden Rule Jones once said it so beautifully: 'What I want for myself I want for everybody."

This is what I want for *myself* – and for *every woman, every mother, and every child in our wonderful world today.*

REFERENCES

Allen James (1903) *As a Man Thinketh and Other Timeless Works,* Wilco

Branch Rickey (1947) American Baseball Coach. Google

Byrne Rhonda (2006) *The Secret,* Beyond Words. Hillsboro Oregon.

Unknown (2012) *Little Eyes Upon You*, Google

Dodd, Mead & Company New York.

Frankl, Viktor (1946) *Man's Search for Meaning.* Verlag fur Jugend und Volk. Austria

Ghandi Mahatma (2 Feb 2021) Google

WHERE IS MY MUMMY?

Hill, Napoleon (1937), *Think and Grow Rich*, The Ralston Society

Hoffer Eric (019) Google

Holliwell Raymond (2004) *Working with the Law*, DeVors & Company

Nightingale Earl (1968) *Lead The Field* . Simon & Schuster Audio/Nightingale-Conant

Proctor Bob (1997) *You Were Born Rich*, Life Success Productions, Cartersville

Smithson Clarence (1997) *You Were Born Rich*, By Bob Proctor. P70

Trine Ralph Waldo (2008) *In Tune With The Infinite*. Arc Manor Maryland.

Troward Thomas (1909) *The Edinburgh Lectures on Mental Science,* Martino Publishing

Waterman Nixon. Mary Mood Poem Google

Mansfield Centre CT

Tzu Lao (Goodreads.

Wattles Wallace D (1910) *The Science of Getting Rich,* Elizabeth Towne Company

AUTHOR'S NOTE

Change has brought us to this place we call ***now.*** Always moving forward to a fuller expression of who we are and our fullest potential.

We have overcome many of the limitations that once stood before us. Our history is now a testimony to the marvellous minds of those who were brave enough to ***change*** their world. What seemed impossible yesterday, is now our everyday experience.

We have conquered our ***outside*** world and now it is the ***time*** to understand and claim our ***inside*** world.

Today we stand at the last frontier, the most exciting the most incredible the most beautiful of all the discoveries that ever have been or ever will be made, the discovery of **who we really are** and ***why*** we were born into this marvellous world.'

Eric Hoffer, the American Philosopher, once said '***the learners of today will inherit the earth whilst the learned will find themselves fully equipped for a world that no longer exists.***'

Now is the time to think in different ways. To take the brave step and choose a better path. Now is the time to take responsibility for our youth who are the product of our past thinking and forge a new pathway for our and their future. The teenagers of today are our leaders of tomorrow.

The old ways of thinking will not change the present issues that challenge us today. Problems cannot be solved at the same level of awareness that created them.

It is of no use, to use the old ways of doing things that are now proving to be of no value. We need to find new ways to reach the hearts and minds of many of this present generation who stand at the precipice of what they see as a lost and forsaken world with no heroes to emulate. In their minds everyone has let them down and they do not trust anymore. They feel like they just 'do not fit in'. They have lost hope. The recklessness by which many of them live their lives is an indication of their lack of consciousness of who they really are and the possibility and power that is within them. They have no faith in anyone or anything. What wasted lives lie before them.

We are responsible for much of the damage that has been done through the choices we made knowingly or unknowingly, and now we are responsible for the restoration.

Change can be challenging, it takes us out of our comfort zone and usually calls from us more than we are prepared to give, but is it worth it? I would say a resounding *yes,* because that is where opportunity awaits us and therein lies our freedom.

Abraham Maslow understood it beautifully when he said **'You will either step forward into Growth or you will step back into Safety.'**

Ultimately the choice lies with us.

As the author of this book my heart's desire is that those who read this book will come to a fuller understanding of how powerful and beautiful is the working of their ***conscious and sub-conscious mind*** and how we can use this awareness to understand and create the desires of our own heart and to add value to the lives of others.

ACKNOWLEDGEMENTS

One does not publish a book all on their own. It is said it takes a village to raise a child and I would say it takes many people to publish a book.

Therefore, I wish to acknowledge some very special people who have been with me on this journey and have contributed to the publishing of this book.

Firstly, to my family. My husband Barry who has been on my side every step of the way, thank you so much. My children and grandchildren who have always given me the encouragement to move forward at a time in my life when it seemed I should be slowing down rather than moving forward. I would like to extend a very special recognition to my granddaughter Sarah Karyn Marks, for without her understanding, patience and never ending help in the world of technology, this book would never have been written. Thank you Sarah for believing in me and encouraging me to keep going.

When one decides to take a particular path in life, we often find that we receive more than we give and, in this instance, I now have new friendships that otherwise I probably would never have discovered and for which I am and will be forever grateful.

Firstly, to Cassandra Willis founder and CEO of Aspire Career Couching, who I have journeyed with over these last three years. It was Cassandra who saw something in me that I never saw in myself. She has been by my side and encouraged me when things got tough. And it was Cassandra who introduced me to my wonderful publisher Karen Weaver for which I will be forever grateful, and I am particularly so grateful to Cassandra for the Forward that she has written in this book.

To Karen Weaver, Publisher, Author, Word Weaver, Docufilm producer, 3xTEDx Speaker, Owner and Executive Director at Senerity Publishing and CEO at MMH Press, thank you for believing in me. It was at my very first meeting with Karen at the end of January this year in Perth that I knew she instantly connected with my heart and understood the words written between the lines of my book. Karen is a weaver of dreams and she has been an ongoing support for me throughout this journey and nothing that I have ever asked of her has been too much trouble.

To Tracey Regan, Business Owner of "All Things Writing" and editor of this book along with Dylan Ingram and Chelsea Wilcox who have been constantly there for me. To Chelsea, a huge thank you for the constant editing of this book. I thank them so much for their attention to detail that has made this publication possible and all those who have formatted, proof read and contributed in so many ways behind the scenes and for keeping my voice and vision alive throughout this journey. I am so grateful for you all.

I am so grateful for the pull on my heart that captured my

attention all those years ago and eventually brought to me the idea of writing this book. It has been spirit who inspired me to write and it has been my constant guide along the way.

Lastly, I thank you my readers who have chosen to take the time to read this book. May it speak to you and inspire you to realise just how incredible you really are. May it bring you peace and true freedom now that you know in the words of the great Ralph Waldo Emerson who you truly are. You are "The Master of your life and the Captain of your Soul."

With Love and Gratitude.
Carole Goodman.

UNDERSTANDING

I have come to bring good news to the poor.
Tell prisoners that they are prisoners no more.
Tell blind people that they can see.
And set the downtrodden free

Luke 4: 17-19

www.ingramcontent.com/pod-product-compliance
Lightning Source LLC
Chambersburg PA
CBHW060614080526
44585CB00013B/822